Laboratory Manual A

Prentice Hall

Biology

Prentice
Hall

Upper Saddle River, New Jersey
Glenview, Illinois
Needham, Massachusetts

Laboratory Manual A

Prentice Hall

Biology

ISBN 0-13-054403-5

1 2 3 4 5 6 7 8 9 10   05 04 03 02 01

Contents

The symbol $\mathcal{P}$ indicates Design-an-Experiment investigations.

Unit 1   The Nature of Life

Chapter 1   The Science of Biology

Chapter 2   The Chemistry of Life

Unit 2   Ecology

Chapter 3   The Biosphere

Chapter 4   Ecosystems and Communities

Chapter 5   Populations

Chapter 6   Humans in the Biosphere

Unit 3   Cells

Unit 4   Genetics

Unit 5   Evolution

Unit 6　Microorganisms and Fungi

Unit 7　Plants

Unit 8　Invertebrates

Unit 9 Chordates

Unit 10 The Human Body

Safety in the Biology Laboratory

Working in the biology laboratory can be interesting, exciting, and rewarding. But it can also be quite dangerous if you are not serious and alert and if proper safety precautions are not taken at all times. You are responsible for maintaining an enjoyable, instructional, and safe environment in the biology laboratory. Unsafe practices endanger not only you but the people around you as well.

Read the following information about safety in the biology laboratory carefully. Review applicable safety information before you begin each Laboratory Investigation. If you have any questions about safety or laboratory procedures, be sure to ask your teacher.

Safety Symbol Guide

All the investigations in this laboratory manual have been designed with safety in mind. If you follow the instructions, you should have a safe and interesting year in the laboratory. Before beginning any investigation, make sure you read the safety rules on pages 8–11 of *Laboratory Manual A*.

The safety symbols shown on page 8 are used throughout *Laboratory Manual A*. They appear first next to the Safety section of an investigation and then next to certain steps in an investigation where specific safety precautions are required. The symbols alert you to the need for special safety precautions. The description of each symbol indicates the precaution(s) you should take whenever you see the symbol in an investigation.

Safety Symbols

These symbols alert you to possible dangers.

Safety Goggles Always wear safety goggles to protect your eyes in any activity involving chemicals, flames, or heating, or the possibility of broken glassware.

Laboratory Apron Wear a laboratory apron to protect your skin and clothing.

Breakage You are working with breakable materials, such as glassware. Handle breakable materials with care. Do not touch broken glassware.

Heat-resistant Gloves Use hand protection when handling hot materials. Hot equipment or hot water can cause burns. Do not touch hot objects with your bare hands.

Plastic Gloves Wear disposable plastic gloves to protect yourself from chemicals or organisms that could be harmful. Keep your hands away from your face. Dispose of the gloves according to your teacher's instructions at the end of the activity.

Heating Use a clamp or tongs to pick up hot glassware. Do not touch hot objects with your bare hands.

Sharp Object Pointed-tip scissors, scalpels, knives, needles, pins, or tacks can cut or puncture your skin. Always direct a sharp edge or point away from yourself and others. Use sharp instruments only as directed.

Electric Shock Avoid the possibility of electric shock. Never use electrical equipment around water, or when equipment is wet or your hands are wet. Be sure cords are untangled and cannot trip anyone. Disconnect the equipment when it is not in use.

Corrosive Chemical Avoid getting acids or other corrosive chemicals on your skin or clothing, or in your eyes. Do not inhale the vapors. Wash your hands when you are finished with the activity.

Poison Do not let any poisonous chemical come in contact with your skin, and do not inhale its vapors. Wash your hands when you are finished with the activity.

Physical Safety When an experiment involves physical activity, take precautions to avoid injuring yourself or others. Follow instructions from your teacher. Alert your teacher if there is any reason you should not participate in the activity.

Animal Safety Treat live animals with care to avoid harming the animals or yourself. Working with animal parts or preserved animals also may require caution. Wash your hands when you are finished.

Plant Safety Handle plants only as directed by your teacher. If you are allergic to certain plants, tell your teacher before doing an activity in which plants are used. Avoid touching poisonous plants or plants with thorns. Wash your hands when you are finished with the activity.

Flames You may be working with flames from a Bunsen burner, candle, or matches. Tie back loose hair and clothing. Follow instructions from your teacher about lighting and extinguishing flames.

No Flames Flammable materials may be present. Make sure no flames, sparks, or exposed heat sources are present.

Fumes When poisonous or unpleasant vapors may be involved, work in a ventilated area. Avoid inhaling vapors directly. Only test an odor when directed to do so by your teacher, and use a wafting motion to direct the vapor toward your nose.

Disposal Chemicals and other used materials must be disposed of safely. Follow the instructions from your teacher.

Hand Washing Wash your hands thoroughly. Use antibacterial soap and warm water. Lather both sides of your hands and between your fingers. Rinse well.

General Safety Awareness You may see this symbol when none of the other symbols appears. In this case, follow the specific instructions provided. You may also see this symbol when you are asked to develop your own procedure. Have your teacher approve your plan before you go further.

Science Safety Rules

One of the first things a scientist learns is that working in the laboratory can be an exciting experience. But the laboratory can also be quite dangerous if proper safety rules are not followed at all times. To prepare yourself for a safe year in the laboratory, read over the following safety rules. Then read them a second time. Make sure you understand each rule. If you do not, ask your teacher to explain any rules you are unsure of.

Dress Code

1. Many materials in the laboratory can cause eye injury. To protect yourself from possible injury, wear safety goggles whenever you are working with chemicals, burners, or any substance that might get into your eyes. Never wear contact lenses in the laboratory.

2. Wear a laboratory apron or coat whenever you are working with chemicals or heated substances.

3. Tie back long hair to keep your hair away from any chemicals, burners and candles, or other laboratory equipment.

4. Remove or tie back any article of clothing or jewelry that can hang down and touch chemicals and flames. Do not wear sandals or open-toed shoes in the laboratory. Never walk around the laboratory barefoot or in stocking feet.

General Safety Rules

5. Be serious and alert when working in the laboratory. Never "horse around" in the laboratory.

6. Be prepared to work when you arrive in the laboratory. Be sure that you understand the procedure to be employed in any laboratory investigation and the possible hazards associated with it.

7. Read all directions for an investigation several times. Follow the directions exactly as they are written. If you are in doubt about any part of the investigation, ask your teacher for assistance.

8. Never perform activities that are not authorized by your teacher. Obtain permission before "experimenting" on your own.

9. Never handle any equipment unless you have specific permission.

10. Take extreme care not to spill any material in the laboratory. If spills occur, ask your teacher immediately about the proper cleanup procedure. Never simply pour chemicals or other substances into the sink or trash container.

11. Never eat or taste anything or apply cosmetics in the laboratory unless directed to do so. This includes food, drinks, candy, and gum, as well as chemicals. Wash your hands before and after performing every investigation.

12. Know the location and proper use of safety equipment such as the fire extinguisher, fire blanket, first-aid kit, safety shower, and eyewash station.

13. Notify your teacher of any medical problems you may have, such as allergies or asthma.

14. Keep your laboratory area clean and free of unnecessary books, papers, and equipment.

First Aid

15. Report all accidents, no matter how minor, to your teacher immediately.

16. Learn what to do in case of specific accidents such as getting acid in your eyes or on your skin. (Rinse acids off your body with lots of water.)

17. Become aware of the location of the first-aid kit. Your teacher should administer any required first aid due to injury. Or your teacher may send you to the school nurse or call a physician.

18. Know where and how to report an accident or fire. Find out the location of the fire extinguisher, phone, and fire alarm. Keep a list of important phone numbers such as the fire department and school

nurse near the phone. Report any fires to your teacher at once.

Heating and Fire Safety

19. Never use a heat source such as a candle or burner without wearing safety goggles.

20. Never heat a chemical you are not instructed to heat. A chemical that is harmless when cool can be dangerous when heated.

21. Maintain a clean work area and keep all materials away from flames.

22. Never reach across a flame.

23. Make sure you know how to light a Bunsen burner. (Your teacher will demonstrate the proper procedure for lighting a burner.) If the flame leaps out of a burner toward you, turn the gas off immediately. Do not touch the burner. It may be hot. And never leave a lighted burner unattended.

24. Point a test tube or bottle that is being heated away from you and others. Chemicals can splash or boil out of a heated test tube.

25. Never heat a liquid in a closed container. The expanding gases produced may blow the container apart, injuring you or others.

26. Never pick up a container that has been heated without first holding the back of your hand near it. If you can feel the heat on the back of your hand, the container may be too hot to handle. Use a clamp, tongs, or heat-resistant gloves when handling hot containers.

Using Chemicals Safely

27. Never mix chemicals for the "fun of it." You might produce a dangerous, possibly explosive, substance.

28. Never touch, taste, or smell a chemical that you do not know for a fact is harmless. Many chemicals are poisonous. If you are instructed to note the fumes in an investigation, gently wave your hand over the opening of a container and direct the fumes toward your nose. Do not inhale the fumes directly from the container.

29. Use only those chemicals needed in the investigation. Keep all lids closed when a chemical is not being used. Notify your teacher whenever chemicals are spilled.

30. Dispose of all chemicals as instructed by your teacher. To avoid contamination, never return chemicals to their original containers.

31. Be extra careful when working with acids or bases. Pour such chemicals over the sink, not over your work bench.

32. When diluting an acid, pour the acid into water. Never pour water into the acid.

33. Rinse any acids off your skin or clothing with water. Immediately notify your teacher of any acid spill.

Using Glassware Safely

34. Never force glass tubing into a rubber stopper. A turning motion and lubricant will be helpful when inserting glass tubing into rubber stoppers or rubber tubing. Your teacher will demonstrate the proper way to insert glass tubing.

35. Never heat glassware that is not thoroughly dry. Use a wire screen to protect glassware from any flame.

36. Keep in mind that hot glassware will not appear hot. Never pick up glassware without first checking to see if it is hot.

37. If you are instructed to cut glass tubing, fire polish the ends immediately to remove sharp edges.

38. Never use broken or chipped glassware. If glassware breaks, notify your teacher and dispose of the glassware in the proper trash container.

39. Never eat or drink from laboratory glassware. Clean glassware thoroughly before putting it away.

Using Sharp Instruments

40. Handle scalpels or razor blades with extreme care. Never cut material toward you; cut away from you.

41. Be careful when handling sharp, pointed objects such as scissors, pins, and dissecting probes.

42. Notify your teacher immediately if you cut yourself or receive a cut.

Handling Living Organisms

43. No investigations that will cause pain, discomfort, or harm to mammals, birds, reptiles, fish, and amphibians should be done in the classroom or at home.

44. Treat all living things with care and respect. Do not touch any organism in the classroom or laboratory unless given permission to do so. Many plants are poisonous or have thorns, and even tame animals may bite or scratch if alarmed.

45. Animals should be handled only if necessary. If an animal is excited or frightened, pregnant, feeding, or with its young, special handling is required.

46. Your teacher will instruct you as to how to handle each species that may be brought into the classroom.

47. Treat all microorganisms as if they were harmful. Use antiseptic procedure, as directed by your teacher, when working with microbes. Dispose of microbes as your teacher directs.

48. Clean your hands thoroughly after handling animals or the cage containing animals.

49. Wear gloves when handling small mammals. Report animal bites or stings to your teacher at once.

End-of-Investigation Rules

50. When an investigation is completed, clean up your work area and return all equipment to its proper place.

51. Wash your hands after every investigation.

52. Turn off all burners before leaving the laboratory. Check that the gas line leading to the burner is off as well.

Safety Contract

Once you have read all the safety information on pages 7–11 in *Laboratory Manual A* and are sure you understand all the rules, fill out the safety contract that follows. Signing this contract tells your teacher that you are aware of the rules of the laboratory. Return your signed contract to your teacher. You will not be allowed to work in the laboratory until you have returned your signed contract.

SAFETY CONTRACT

I, _____, have read the

Safety in the Biology Laboratory section on pages 7–11 in *Biology*

Laboratory Manual A. I understand its contents completely, and agree to

follow all the safety rules and guidelines that have been established in

each of the following areas:

(please check)

☐ Dress Code   ☐ Using Glassware Safely

☐ General Safety Rules   ☐ Using Sharp Instruments

☐ First Aid   ☐ Handling Living Organisms

☐ Heating and Fire Safety   ☐ End-of-Investigation Rules

☐ Using Chemicals Safely

Signature _____ Date _____

How to Use the Laboratory Manual

This is probably the most exciting time in history to be studying biology. The science of biology is progressing rapidly. Biology is directly related to many of today's most important news stories. Cloning of animals; AIDS; animal rights; genetic fingerprinting; acid rain; and efforts to save endangered species all depend on biology.

In order to gain a working knowledge of biology, you need to understand some of the processes that scientists use to find answers to problems. The Laboratory Investigations and activities in *Laboratory Manual A* enable you to learn about and practice methods used by scientists in their quest to increase human knowledge.

In each Laboratory Investigation, your objective is to solve a problem using scientific methods. Each Laboratory Investigation follows a standard outline that will help you tackle the problem in a systematic and organized manner. One Laboratory Investigation in each unit (except Unit 1) is a Design an Experiment activity that follows a slightly different outline.

Introduction The Introduction provides information you will need to complete the investigation, and ties the Laboratory Investigation to concepts discussed in the textbook. The Introduction corresponds to the first step in any scientific work—gathering information about the topic so that you can develop a hypothesis.

Problem This section presents a problem in the form of a question. Your job is to solve the problem based on your observations.

Pre-Lab Discussion After reading the Laboratory Investigation, answering the questions in this section will help you to clarify the purpose of the investigation. By asking you the reasons for specific steps in the Procedure, this section prepares you to carry out the Laboratory Investigation. Questions in this section may also highlight safety concerns to which you should pay careful attention.

Materials A list of all required materials appears at the beginning of the investigation. The quantity of material for each investigation is indicated for individual students, pairs of students, or groups of students.

Safety The Safety section warns you of potential hazards and tells you about precautions you should take to decrease the risk of accidents. The safety symbols that are relevant to the Laboratory Investigation appear next to the title of the Safety section. They also appear next to certain steps of the Procedure.

Procedure This section provides detailed step-by-step instructions. Diagrams are included where necessary. The Procedure enables you to test the hypothesis.

Make sure you read the entire Procedure carefully before you begin the investigation. Look for safety symbols and notes. If safety symbols appear next to a step in the Procedure, you should follow the corresponding safety precaution(s) for that step and all following steps. **CAUTION** statements within the steps of the Procedure warn of possible hazards. **Notes** in the Procedure provide special directions.

In keeping with scientific methods, you will record your data by filling in data tables, graphing data, labeling diagrams, drawing observed structures, and answering questions.

Analysis and Conclusions Two steps of the scientific method—analyzing data and forming a conclusion—are represented in this section. Here, you are to analyze and interpret your experimental results. This section may also challenge you to apply your conclusions to real-life situations or related experiments.

Going Further This section suggests additional activities for you to pursue on your own. Some of these are extensions of the Laboratory Investigation that you might perform with your teacher's permission. Others involve library research.

Presenting Data

To seek answers to problems or questions they have about the world, scientists typically perform many experiments in the laboratory. In doing so, they observe physical characteristics and processes, select areas for study, and review the scientific literature to gain background information about the topic they are investigating. They then form hypotheses, test these hypotheses through controlled experiments, record and analyze data, and develop a conclusion about the correctness of the hypotheses. Finally, they report their findings in detail, giving enough information about their experimental procedure so that other scientists are able to replicate the experiments and verify the results.

The Laboratory Investigations in *Laboratory Manual A* provide an opportunity for you to investigate scientific problems in the same manner as that of a typical scientist. As you perform these investigations, you will employ many of the techniques and steps of the scientific method a working scientist does. Some of the most important skills you will acquire are associated with the step of the scientific method known as recording and analyzing data. Three of these skills are creating and filling in data tables, making drawings, and finding averages. Another set of skills useful in presenting data is examined in the Laboratory Skills activity titled Using Graphing Skills.

It is important to record data precisely—even if the results of an investigation appear to be wrong. And it is extremely important to keep in mind that developing laboratory skills and data analysis skills is actually more valuable than simply arriving at the correct answers. If you analyze your data correctly—even if the data are not perfect— you will be learning to think as a scientist thinks. And that is the purpose of this laboratory manual and your experience in the biology laboratory.

Data Tables

When scientists conduct various experiments and do research, they collect vast amounts of information: for example, measurements, descriptions, and other observations. To communicate and interpret this information, they must record it in an organized fashion. Scientists use data tables for this purpose.

You will be responsible for completing data tables for many of the Laboratory Investigations. Each column in a data table has a heading. The column headings explain where particular data are to be placed. The completed data tables will help you interpret the information you collected and answer the questions found at the end of each Laboratory Investigation.

Name_____ Class_____ Date _____

EXERCISE 1

Given the following information, complete Data Table 1. Then interpret the data and answer the five questions that follow.

Information: The following hair colors were found among three classes of students:

Class 1: brown— 20   Class 2: brown— 18   Class 3: brown— 15
         black— 1   black— 0   black— 4
         blond— 4   blond— 6   blond— 15

Data Table

Hair Color	Class 1	Class 2	Class 3	Total
Brown				
Black				
Blond				

1. What type of information is being gathered?

_____

_____

2. Which hair color occurs most often?

_____

_____

3. From the information in the Data Table, can you give the number of boys with black hair?

_____

4. What information can you give about the number of students with black hair?

_____

5. Which class has the most blond students?

_____

_____

6. How many students made up the entire student population?

_____

_____

EXERCISE 2

Given the following information, organize the data into a table. Use the blank area provided in Figure 1 to draw in the necessary columns and rows. Then interpret the data and answer the questions that follow.

Information: On an expedition around the world, several scientists collected the venom of various snakes. One of the tests that the scientists conducted determined the toxicity of the venom of each snake. Other data obtained by the scientists included the mortality percentage, or relative death rate, from the bites of various snakes.

The snakes observed were the (1) southern United States copperhead, (2) western diamondback rattlesnake, (3) eastern coral snake, (4) king cobra, (5) Indian krait, (6) European viper, (7) bushmaster, (8) fer-de-lance, (9) black-necked cobra, (10) puff adder.

The mortality percentage of people bitten by the snakes varied from 100% to less than 1%. The scientists noted the mortality percentage for each of the snakes was (1) less than 1%, (2) 5–15%, (3) 5–20%, (4) greater than 40%, (5) 77%, (6) 1–5%, (7) usually 100%, (8) 10–20%, (9) 11–40%, and (10) 11–40%.

Figure 1

1. Which snake's venom has the highest mortality rate?

2. Which snake's venom has the lowest mortality rate?

3. From the information recorded, can you determine the snake whose venom works the most rapidly? The least rapidly?

4. Which two snakes' venom have the same mortality rate?

5. How many types of snakes were observed?

DRAWINGS

Laboratory drawings can be made using several methods. Some drawings are made in circles that represent the viewing field of a microscope or another type of magnifier. When completing these drawings, be sure to include the magnification at which you viewed the object. Other laboratory drawings represent organisms or parts of organisms. These drawings show the relative size, shape, and location of anatomical structures. When completing representative drawings, make the structures as clear and as accurate as possible.

Most laboratory drawings are labeled. Use the following guidelines to help make your laboratory drawings clear and legible.

- Use a ruler to draw label lines.
- Label lines should point to the center of the structure being labeled.
- Do not write on the label lines.
- Print all labels horizontally.
- Label the right-hand side of the drawing, if possible.
- Do not cross label lines.

EXERCISE 3

The following drawing was made without using the guidelines above. Circle those parts of the drawing that do not follow the guidelines. Then, on the lines provided, explain how the drawing should be done.

Magnification _____

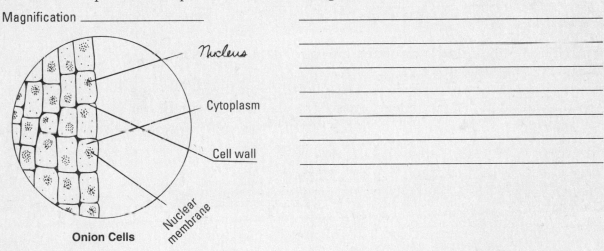

Onion Cells

Figure 2

AVERAGES

Occasionally you will be required to find the average of data gathered from an investigation. To find an average, add the items in the group together and then divide the total by the number of items. For example, if there were five students of different ages—12, 13, 14, 17, and 19—how would you find the average age of the group? Add the five ages together and divide the total by 5, which is the number of items (students) in the group. What is the average age of this group of students? Your answer should be 15 years old.

EXERCISE 4

In a garden the heights of six sunflowers are 135 cm, 162.5 cm, 180 cm, 235 cm, 185 cm, and 167.5 cm. What is the average height of the sunflowers?

_____

EXERCISE 5

Find the average for the following group of data. Then use the results to answer the questions that follow.

   In an experiment on plant growth and overcrowding, plants of the following heights are in three equal-sized containers.

Flowerpot 1:   20.0 cm and 18.2 cm
Flowerpot 2:   12 cm, 10.8 cm, 11.2 cm, and 12.4 cm
Flowerpot 3:   7.5 cm, 8.0 cm, 6.0 cm, 6.2 cm, 5.8 cm, and 7.3 cm

1. What is the average height of the plants in each flowerpot?

   _____

   _____

2. In which flowerpot did the plants grow the tallest? Explain.

   _____

   _____

EXERCISE 6

Find the averages for the following groups of data. Express your answers to the nearest tenth.

   In a sample group of students, the number of breaths per minute was measured at rest and after exercise. The results were as follows:

At rest
Males: 10.1, 13, 12.5, 10.2, 13.1, 11.8
Females: 10.4, 13.0, 12.1, 11.9, 10.5, 12.8

After exercise
Males: 18.9, 23.7, 22.6, 21.3, 19.2, 20.6
Females: 25, 26.7, 29, 35.3, 33.1, 31.7

1. What is the average number of breaths per minute for males at rest? _____
   Females at rest? _____
2. What is the average number of breaths per minute for males after exercise? _____
   Females after exercise? _____
3. How many students make up the sample group? _____
4. What is the average number of breaths per minute for the entire group at rest? _____
   After exercise? _____
5. Do males or females take more breaths per minute at rest? _____
   After exercise? _____

Recognizing Laboratory Safety

Introduction

An important part of your study of biology will be working in a laboratory. In the laboratory, you and your classmates will learn biology by actively conducting and observing experiments. Working directly with living things will provide opportunities for you to better understand the principles of biology discussed in your textbook or talked about in class.

Most of the laboratory work you will do is quite safe. However, some laboratory equipment, chemicals, and specimens can be dangerous if handled improperly. Laboratory accidents do not just happen. They are caused by carelessness, improper handling of equipment and specimens, or inappropriate behavior.

In this investigation, you will learn how to prevent accidents and thus work safely in a laboratory. You will review some safety guidelines and become acquainted with the location and proper use of safety equipment in your classroom laboratory.

Problem

What are the proper practices for working safely in a biology laboratory?

Pre-Lab Discussion

Read the entire investigation. Then, work with a partner to answer the following questions.

1. Why might eating or drinking in the laboratory be dangerous?

   _____

   _____

   _____

2. How can reading through the entire laboratory before beginning the Procedure help prevent accidents?

   _____

   _____

   _____

3. Look around the room. What safety equipment do you recognize?

   _____

4. What safety procedures should you follow when cleaning up at the end of a lab?

   _____

5. Can minor safety procedures be skipped in order to finish the lab before the bell rings?

   _____

Materials *(per group)*

Biology textbook
Laboratory safety equipment (for demonstration)

Procedure

1. Carefully read the list of laboratory safety rules listed in Appendix B of your textbook.

2. Special symbols are used throughout this laboratory manual to call attention to investigations that require extra caution. Use Appendix B in your textbook as a reference to describe what each symbol printed below means.

1. _____
_____

2. _____
_____

3. _____
_____

4. _____
_____

5. _____
_____

6. _____
_____

7. _____
_____

8. _____
_____

Name_____ Class_____ Date _____

3. Your teacher will point out the location of the safety equipment in your classroom laboratory. Pay special attention to instructions for using such equipment as fire extinguishers, eyewash fountains, fire blankets, safety showers, and items in first-aid kits. Use the space provided below to list the location of all safety equipment in your laboratory.

_____
_____
_____
_____
_____

Analysis and Conclusions

Observing Look at each of the following drawings and explain why the laboratory activities pictured are unsafe.

1. _____
_____
_____
_____
_____
_____
_____

2. _____
_____
_____
_____
_____
_____
_____

3. _____
_____
_____
_____
_____
_____
_____

4. _____

_____

_____

_____

_____

_____

_____

Going Further

Many houseplants and some plants found in biology laboratories are poisonous. Use appropriate library resources to do research on several common poisonous plants. Share your research with your classmates. You may prepare a booklet describing common poisonous plants. Use drawings or photographs to illustrate your booklet.

Identifying Laboratory Equipment

Introduction

Scientists use a variety of tools to explore the world around them. Tools are very important in the advancement of science. The type of tools scientists use depends on the problems they are trying to solve. A scientist may use something as simple as a metric ruler to measure the length of a leaf. At another time, the same scientist may use a complex computer to analyze large amounts of data concerning hundreds of leaves.

In this investigation, you will identify pieces of laboratory equipment likely to be found in a biology laboratory. You will also learn the function of each piece of laboratory equipment.

Problem

What are the names and functions of some of the pieces of laboratory equipment found in a typical biology laboratory?

Pre-Lab Discussion

Read the entire investigation. Then, work with a partner to answer the following questions.

1. What kinds of measurements might you need to make in the laboratory?

_____

2. What kinds of equipment would you need for these tasks?

_____

3. Why are there several types of glassware marked for measuring?

_____

_____

_____

4. How might glassware be used differently?

_____

_____

_____

5. When might you need to use a thermometer in the lab?

_____

_____

Safety

Handle all glassware carefully. Be careful when handling sharp instruments. Always handle the microscope with extreme care. You are responsible for its proper care and use. Use caution when handling glass slides as they can break easily and cut you. Note all safety alert symbols next to the steps in the Procedure and review the meanings of each symbol by referring to Safety Symbols on page 8.

Procedure

1. Look at the drawings of the laboratory equipment in Figure 1. In the space provided, write the name of each piece of laboratory equipment.

2. Carefully inspect the different types of laboratory equipment that have been set out by your teacher. In the space provided write the function of each piece of laboratory equipment.

A. _____

B. _____

C. _____

D. _____

E. _____

F. _____

G. _____

H. _____

I. _____

J. _____

K. _____

L. _____

M. _____

N. _____

O. _____

P. _____

Q. _____

R. _____

S. _____

T. _____

U. _____

V. _____

W. _____

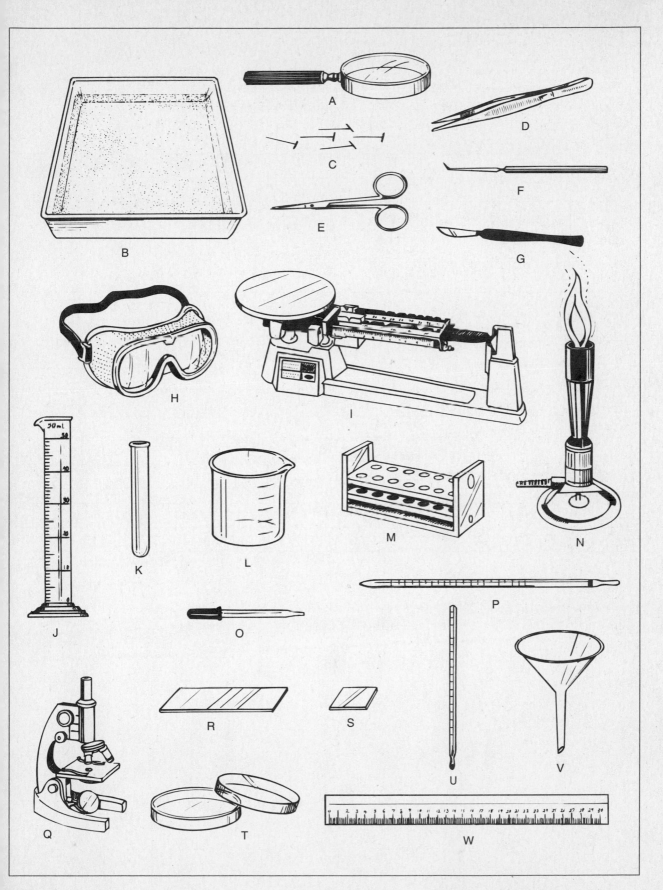

Figure 1

Analysis and Conclusions

1. **Classifying** Which laboratory tools can be used to magnify small objects so they can be seen more easily?

_____

2. **Classifying** Which laboratory tools are useful when looking at the internal organs of an earthworm?

_____

_____

_____

3. **Applying Concepts** What tool or tools would you use to make each of the following measurements?

   a. amount of milk in a small glass

   _____

   b. length of a sheet of paper

   _____

   c. temperature of a swimming pool

   _____

   d. mass of a baseball

   _____

4. **Drawing Conclusions** How do laboratory tools improve the observations made by a scientist?

   _____

   _____

   _____

Going Further

Examine other types of laboratory equipment that you will be using in the biology laboratory. Try to determine the function of each piece of equipment.

Making Metric Measurements

Introduction

In many biology investigations, precise measurements must be made before observations can be interpreted. For everyday measuring, we still use English units such as the inch, quart, and pound. For scientific work, and for everyday measuring in most countries, the International System of Units (SI) is used. Eventually our country will use SI units for everyday measuring too.

Like our money system, SI is a metric system. All units are based on the number 10. In the SI system it is easy to change one unit to another because all units are related to one another by a power of 10.

In this investigation, you will review SI units for measuring length, liquid volume, and mass. You will also learn how to use some common laboratory equipment used for measuring.

Problem

How are metric units of measurement used in the laboratory?

Pre-Lab Discussion

Read the entire investigation. Then, work with a partner to answer the following questions.

1. Why do scientists and other people in most countries use the metric system for measurements?

   _____

   _____

2. Why is it easy to change from one unit to another in the SI system?

   _____

3. What connections can you identify between the metric units for length and volume?

   _____

   _____

   _____

   _____

4. Why is it difficult to convert miles to yards or feet?

   _____

   _____

5. Name several aspects of everyday life that will change when our country converts to SI units.

   _____

   _____

Materials *(per group)*

meterstick

metric ruler

small test tube

rubber stopper

coin

triple-beam balance

50-mL beaker

100-mL graduated cylinder

Safety 🔲🔲

Handle all glassware carefully. Note all safety alert symbols next to the steps in the Procedure and review the meanings of each symbol by referring to Safety Symbols on page 8.

Procedure

Part A. Measuring Length

1. Use the meterstick to measure the length, width, and height of your laboratory table or desk in meters. Record your measurements to the nearest hundredth of a meter in Data Table 1.

2. Convert the measurements from meters to centimeters and then to millimeters. Record these measurements in Data Table 1.

3. Use a metric ruler to measure the length of a small test tube and the diameter of its mouth in centimeters. Record your measurements to the nearest millimeter in Data Table 2.

4. Convert the measurements from centimeters to millimeters. Record these measurements in Data Table 2.

Data Table 1

Lab Table Measurements			
Dimension	m	cm	mm
Length			
Width			
Height			

Data Table 2

Test Tube Measurements		
Dimension	cm	mm
Length		
Diameter of mouth		

Part B. Measuring the Volume of a Liquid

 1. Fill the test tube to the top with water. Pour the water into the graduated cylinder.

2. The surface of the liquid will be slightly curved. This curved surface is called a meniscus. To measure the volume accurately, your eye must be at the same level as the bottom of the meniscus. See Figure 1. Record the volume of the water from the test tube to the nearest milliliter in Data Table 3.

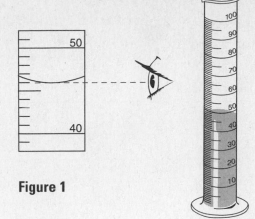

Figure 1

Data Table 3

Measurement of Volume	
Object	Volume (mL)
Water in test tube	

Part C. Measuring Mass

 1. Place the 50-mL beaker on the pan of the balance. Be sure that the riders on the triple-beam balance are moved all the way to the left and that the pointer rests on zero. See Figure 2.

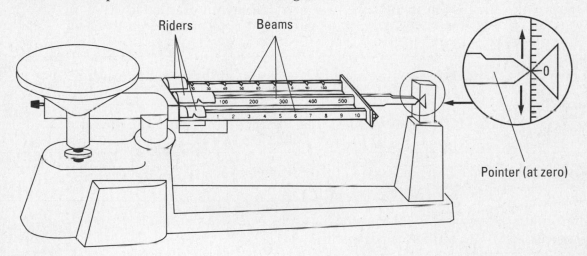

Figure 2

2. Move the rider on the middle beam to the right one notch at a time until the pointer drops below zero. Move the rider back one notch.

3. Move the rider on the back beam one notch at a time until the pointer again drops below zero. Move the rider back one notch.

4. Slide the rider along the front beam until the pointer stops at zero. The mass of the object is equal to the sum of the readings on the three beams.

5. Record the mass of the beaker to the nearest tenth of a gram in Data Table 4. Remove the beaker.

6. Repeat steps 2 through 5 using the rubber stopper and then the coin.

7. Use the graduated cylinder to place exactly 40 mL of water in the beaker. Determine the combined mass of the beaker and water. Record this mass to the nearest tenth of a gram in Data Table 4.

Data Table 4

Measurement of Mass	
Object	Mass (g)
50-mL beaker	
Rubber stopper	
Coin	
50-mL beaker plus 40 mL of water	

Analysis and Conclusions

1. **Calculating** How do you convert meters to centimeters? Centimeters to millimeters?

2. **Observing** What is the largest volume of liquid your graduated cylinder can measure?

3. **Observing** What is the smallest volume of a liquid your graduated cylinder can measure?

4. **Calculating** What is the largest mass of an object your balance can measure?

5. **Observing** What is the smallest mass of an object your balance can measure?

6. **Calculating** What is the mass of 40 mL of water?

7. **Predicting** How would you find the mass of a certain amount of water that you poured into a paper cup?

8. **Calculating** In this investigation you found the mass of 40 mL of water. Based on your observations, what is the mass of 1 mL of water?

Going Further

If other types of laboratory balances are available, such as an electronic balance or a double-pan balance, use them to find the masses of several different objects. Compare the accuracy of the different balances.

Applying the Scientific Method

Introduction

The scientific method is a procedure used to gather information and test ideas. Scientists use the scientific method to answer questions about life and living organisms. Experimentation is an important part of the scientific method. In order to ensure that the results of an experiment are due to the variable being tested, a scientist must have both an experimental setup and a control setup. The experimental setup and the control setup differ only in the variable being tested.

In this investigation, you will form a hypothesis, test it, and draw a conclusion based on your observations.

Problem

Is light necessary for the sprouting of a potato?

Pre-Lab Discussion

Read the entire investigation. Then, work with a partner to answer the following questions.

1. Under what conditions do potatoes usually grow?

_____

2. Why is it important to seal the plastic bags?

_____

3. How does cutting one potato in half help limit the variables of the experiment?

_____

_____

4. Why is it necessary to keep both potato halves on moist paper towels?

_____

5. What evidence will tell you whether or not light is necessary for sprouting a potato?

_____

Materials *(per group)*

1 medium-sized potato
2 plastic bags with twist ties
knife
2 paper towels

Safety

Put on a laboratory apron if one is available. Be careful when handling sharp instruments. Note all safety alert symbols next to the steps in the Procedure and review the meanings of each symbol by referring to Safety Symbols on page 8.

Procedure

1. With the members of your group, discuss whether or not the potato needs light to sprout. Based on your discussion, record your hypothesis in the space provided.

2. Carefully cut the potato in half lengthwise. Count the number of eyes on the potato half to be put in the dark and the half to be put in the light. Record this information in Data Table 1.
   Hypothesis

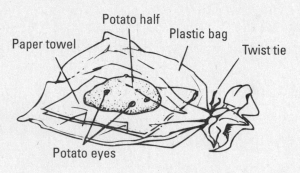

Figure 1

3. Fold each paper towel repeatedly until you have a rectangle about the same size as your potato halves. Moisten the towels with water. Place a folded paper towel in each plastic bag.

4. Place a potato half in each plastic bag with the cut surface on the paper towel. Tie each bag with a twist tie. See Figure 1.

5. Place one of the plastic bags in a place that receives light. Place the other plastic bag in a dark place. Be sure that the potato halves remain on top of the paper towels and that both potato halves are kept at the same temperature.

6. After one week, open each plastic bag and count the number of sprouts. Record this information in the Data Table.

7. To calculate the percentage of eyes sprouting, divide the number of sprouts by the number of eyes and multiply the result by 100. Record your answers in the Data Table.

8. Have one person from your group go to the chalkboard to record your group's data in the table that has been drawn by your teacher.

Data Table 3

	Number of Eyes	Number of Sprouts	Percentage of Eyes Sprouting
Potato half in dark			
Potato half in light			

Analysis and Conclusions

1. **Observing** Did more sprouts grow in the light or in the dark?

_____

2. **Controlling Variables** What was the control setup in this investigation?

_____

_____

3. **Controlling Variables** What was the experimental setup in this investigation?

_____

4. **Drawing Conclusions** What conclusion can you draw from this investigation?

_____

5. **Evaluating and Revising** How does your hypothesis compare with your results after completing the investigation?

_____

_____

_____

6. **Controlling Variables** Why was it important to keep both the control setup and the experimental setup at the same temperature throughout the experiment?

_____

_____

_____

7. **Inferring** How do you know that the control setup and the experimental setup were not at the same temperature during the day?

_____

Going Further

Devise an experiment to see if another variable, such as temperature or water, affects the number of sprouts a potato produces.

Laboratory Skills 5

Using a Compound Light Microscope

Introduction

Many objects are too small to be seen by the eye alone. They can be seen, however, with the use of an instrument that magnifies, or visually enlarges, the object. One such instrument, which is of great importance to biologists and other scientists, is the compound light microscope. A compound light microscope consists of a light source or mirror that illuminates the object to be observed, an objective lens that magnifies the image of the object, and an eyepiece (ocular lens) that further magnifies the image of the object and projects it into the viewer's eye.

Objects, or specimens, to be observed under a microscope are generally prepared in one of two ways. Prepared or permanent slides are made to last a long time. They are usually purchased from biological supply houses. Temporary or wet mount slides are made to last only a short time—usually one laboratory period.

The microscope is an expensive precision instrument that requires special care and handling. In this investigation, you will learn the parts of a compound light microscope, the functions of those parts, and the proper use and care of the microscope. You will also learn the technique of preparing wet-mount slides.

Problem

What is the proper use of a compound light microscope?

Pre-Lab Discussion

Read the entire investigation. Then, work with a partner to answer the following questions.

1. Why might it be a good idea to keep your microscope at least 10 cm from the edge of the table?

_____

2. Why should a microscope slide and coverslip be held by their edges?

_____

_____

3. Why do scientists use microscopes?

_____

4. Why should you use lens paper only once?

_____

_____

5. Why is it important to eliminate air bubbles from the slide?

_____

Materials *(per group)*

compound light microscope
prepared slide
lens paper
soft cloth (or cheesecloth)
newspaper

microscope slide
coverslip
dissecting probe
dropper pipette
scissors

Safety 🧤🔬🔥

Put on a laboratory apron if one is available. Always handle the microscope with extreme care. You are responsible for its proper care and use. Use caution when handling microscope slides as they can break easily and cut you. Never use direct sunlight as a light source for a compound light microscope. The sunlight reflecting through the microscope could damage your eye. Be careful when handling sharp instruments. Observe proper laboratory procedures when using electrical equipment. Note all safety alert symbols next to the steps in the Procedure and review the meanings of each symbol by referring to Safety Symbols on page 8.

Procedure

Part A. Care of the Compound Light Microscope

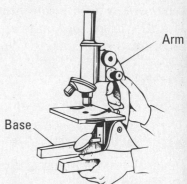

Figure 1

1. Figure 1 shows the proper way to carry a microscope. Always carry the microscope with both hands. Grasp the arm of the microscope with one hand and place your other hand under the base. Always hold the microscope in an upright position so that the eyepiece cannot fall out. Place a microscope on your worktable or desk at least 10 cm from the edge. Position the microscope with the arm facing you.

2. Notice the numbers etched on the objectives and on the eyepiece. Each number is followed by an "X" that means "times." For example, the low-power objective may have the number "10X" on its side, as shown in Figure 2. That objective magnifies an object 10 times its normal size. Record the magnifications of your microscope in the Data Table. The total magnification of a microscope is calculated by multiplying the magnification of the objective by the magnification of the eyepiece. For example:

magnification of objective		magnification of eyepiece		total magnification
	×		=	
10X	×	10X	=	100X

Use the formula to complete the Data Table.

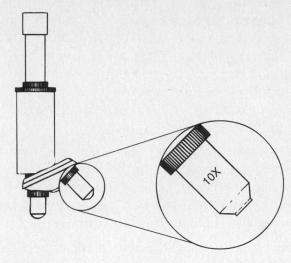

Figure 2

Data Table

Objective	Magnification of Objective	Magnification of Eyepiece	Total Magnification
Low power			
High power			
Other			

4. Before you use the microscope, clean the lenses of the objectives and eyepiece with lens paper. **Note:** *To avoid scratching the lenses, never clean or wipe them with anything other than lens paper. Use a new piece of lens paper on each lens you clean. Never touch a lens with your finger. The oils on your skin may attract dust or lint that could scratch the lens.*

Part B. Use of a Compound Light Microscope

1. Look at the microscope from the side. Locate the coarse adjustment knob which moves the objectives up and down. Practice moving the coarse adjustment knob to see how it moves the objectives with each turn.

2. Turn the coarse adjustment so that the low-power objective is positioned about 3 cm from the stage. Locate the revolving nosepiece. Turn the nosepiece until you hear the high-power objective click into position. See Figure 3. When an objective clicks into position, it is in the proper alignment for light to pass from the light source through the objective into the viewer's eye. Now turn the nosepiece until the low-power objective clicks back into position. **Note:** *Always look at the microscope from the side when moving an objective so that the microscope does not hit or damage the slide.*

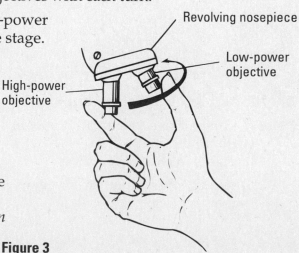

Revolving nosepiece

Low-power objective

High-power objective

Figure 3

3. If your microscope has an electric light source, plug in the cord and turn on the light. If your microscope has a mirror, turn the mirror toward a light source such as a desk lamp or window. **CAUTION:** *Never use the sun as a direct source of light.* Look through the eyepiece. Adjust the diaphragm to permit sufficient light to enter the microscope. The white circle of light you see is the field of view. If your microscope has a mirror, move the mirror until the field of view is evenly illuminated.

4. Place a prepared slide on the stage so that it is centered over the stage opening. Use the stage clips to hold the slide in position. Turn the low-power objective into place. Look at the microscope from the side and turn the coarse adjustment so that the low-power objective is as close as possible to the stage without touching it.

5. Look through the eyepiece and turn the coarse adjustment to move the low-power objective away from the stage until the object comes into focus. To avoid eyestrain, keep both eyes open while looking through a microscope. **CAUTION:** *To avoid moving the objective into the slide, never lower the objective toward the stage while looking through the eyepiece.*

6. Turn the fine adjustment to bring the object into sharp focus. You may wish to adjust the diaphragm so that you can see the object more clearly. In the appropriate space below, draw what you see through the microscope. Note the magnification.

7. Look at the microscope from the side and rotate the nosepiece until the high-power objective clicks into position. Look through the eyepiece. Turn the fine adjustment to bring the object on the slide into focus. **CAUTION:** *Never use the coarse adjustment when focusing the high-power objective lens. This could break your slide or damage the lens.* In the appropriate space below, draw what you see through the microscope. Note the magnification.

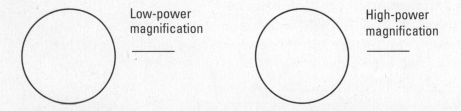

Low-power magnification

High-power magnification

8. Remove the slide. Move the low-power objective into position.

Part C. Preparing a Wet Mount

1. Use a pair of scissors to cut a letter "e" from a piece of newspaper. Cut out the smallest letter "e" you can find. Position the "e" on the center of a clean glass slide.

2. Use a dropper pipette to place one drop of water on the cut piece of newspaper. See Figure 4B.

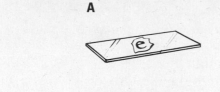

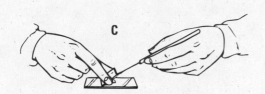

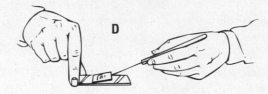

Figure 4

3. Hold a clean coverslip in your fingers as shown in Figure 4C. Make sure the bottom edge of the coverslip is in the drop of water. Use a dissecting needle to slowly lower the coverslip onto the wet newspaper. Slowly lowering the coverslip prevents air bubbles from being trapped between the slide and the coverslip. The type of slide you have just made is called a wet mount. Practice making a wet mount until you can do so without trapping air bubbles on the slide.

4. Center the wet mount on the stage with the letter "e" in its normal upright position. **Note:** *Make sure the bottom of the slide is dry before you place it on the stage.* Turn the low-power objective into position and bring the "e" into focus. In the appropriate place below, draw the letter "e" as seen through the microscope. Note the magnification.

5. While looking through the eyepiece, move the slide to the left. Notice the way the letter seems to move. Now move the slide to the right. Again notice the way the letter seems to move. Move the slide up and down and observe the direction the letter moves.

6. Turn the high-power objective into position and bring the letter "e" into focus. In the appropriate place below, draw the letter "e" as seen through the microscope. Note the magnification.

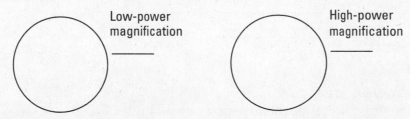

7. Take apart the wet mount. Clean the slide and coverslip with soap and water. Carefully dry the slide and coverslip with paper towels and return them to their boxes.

8. Rotate the low-power objective into position and use the coarse adjustment to place it as close to the stage as possible without touching. Carefully pick up the microscope and return it to its storage area.

Analysis and Conclusions

1. Inferring Why do you place one hand under the base of the microscope as you carry it?

_____

2. Observing How is the image of an object seen through the high-power objective different from the image seen through the low-power objective?

_____

_____

_____

3. Observing How does the letter "e" as seen through the microscope differ from the way an "e" normally appears?

_____

_____

4. Inferring Explain why a specimen to be viewed under the microscope must be thin.

_____

_____

_____

5. Inferring Why should you never use coarse adjustment when focusing the high-power objective lens?

_____

_____

6. Drawing Conclusions Suppose you were observing an organism through the microscope and noticed that it moved toward the bottom of the slide and then it moved to the right. What does this tell you about the actual movement of the organism?

_____

_____

_____

_____

Going Further

View some common objects, such as thread or a small piece of a color photograph from a magazine under the low-power and high-power objectives of the microscope. Make a drawing for each object. Describe the appearance of the objects when viewed under a microscope.

Laboratory Skills 6

Using the Bunsen Burner

Introduction

Sometimes a biologist needs to heat materials. In the laboratory, one of the most efficient ways to do this is to use a Bunsen burner. Bunsen burners are made in a variety of designs. In every one, however, a mixture of air and gas is burned. In most Bunsen burners, the amounts of air and gas can be controlled. In some laboratories, electric hot plates or portable gas burners are used instead of Bunsen burners.

In this investigation, you will learn the parts of the Bunsen burner and their functions. You will also learn how to use the Bunsen burner safely in the laboratory.

Problem

How can the Bunsen burner be safely used to heat materials in the laboratory?

Pre-Lab Discussion

Read the entire investigation. Then, work with a partner to answer the following questions.

1. Why is it important to wear safety goggles when using a Bunsen burner?

   _____

   _____

2. Why is it important to tie back loose hair and clothing when using a Bunsen burner?

   _____

   _____

3. In addition to the items mentioned in questions 1 and 2, what other safety precautions should be followed before lighting a Bunsen burner?

   _____

   _____

   _____

4. How is using a Bunsen burner different from using a candle?

   _____

   _____

   _____

5. Why is it important to make sure that the volume of water and the starting temperature are the same in each trial?

   _____

   _____

Name_____ Class_____ Date _____

Materials *(per group)*

Bunsen burner

ring stand

2 250-mL beakers

wire gauze

metric ruler

beaker tongs

iron ring

100-mL graduated cylinder

flint striker or matches

clock with second hand

Safety 🦺 🧤 🔥 🧤 ✋

Put on a laboratory apron if one is available. Put on safety goggles. Handle all glassware carefully. Tie back loose hair and clothing when using the Bunsen burner. Use extreme care when working with heated equipment or materials to avoid burns. Note all safety alert symbols next to the steps in the Procedure and review the meanings of each symbol by referring to Safety Symbols on page 8.

Procedure

1. Examine your burner when it is *not* connected to the gas outlet. If your burner is the type that can easily be taken apart, unscrew the barrel from the base and locate the parts shown in Figure 1. As you examine the parts, think about their functions.

   • The barrel is the area where the air and gas mix.

   • The collar can be turned to adjust the intake of air. If you turn the collar so that the holes are larger, more air will be drawn into the barrel.

   • The air intake openings are the holes in the collar through which air is drawn in.

   • The base supports the burner so that it does not tip over.

   • The gas intake tube brings the supply of gas from the outlet to the burner.

   • The spud is the small opening through which the gas flows. The small opening causes the gas to enter with great speed.

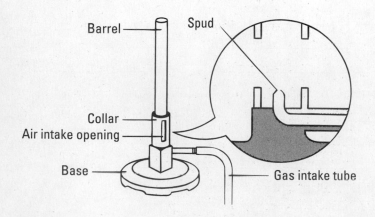

Figure 1

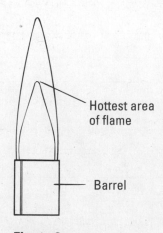

Figure 2

2. Reassemble the Bunsen burner if necessary and connect the gas intake tube to the gas outlet. **CAUTION:** *Put on safety goggles.* Make sure that the burner is placed away from flammable materials.

3. Adjust the collar so that the air intake openings are half open. If you use a match to light the burner, light the match and hold it about 2 cm above and just to the right of the barrel. Hold the match in this position while you open the gas outlet valve slowly until it is fully open. **CAUTION:** *To avoid burns on your hands, always use extreme care when handling lighted matches.* The burner can also be turned off by using the valve. Do not lean over the burner when lighting it.

4. If you use a flint striker to light the burner, hold the striker in the same position you would hold a lighted match. To light the burner with a striker, you must produce a spark at the same time you open the gas valve.

5. Practice lighting the burner several times. Every member of your group should be given the opportunity to light the burner.

6. The most efficient and hottest flame is blue in color and has distinct regions as shown in Figure 2. Adjust the collar so that the flame is blue and a pale blue inner cone is visible.

7. Adjust the flow of gas until the flame is about 6 cm high. Some burners have a valve in the base to regulate the flow of gas, but the flow of gas can always be adjusted at the gas outlet valve. After adjusting the flow of gas, shut off the burner. Leave your safety goggles on for the remainder of the investigation.

8. Arrange the apparatus as pictured in Figure 3.

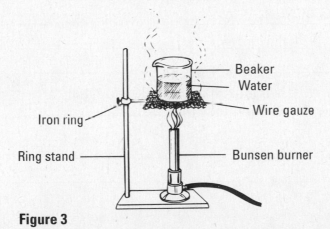

Figure 3

9. Adjust the iron ring so that the bottom of the beaker is about 2 cm above the mouth of the burner barrel. Measure 100 mL of water in the graduated cylinder and pour it into one of the beakers.

10. Light the burner and heat the beaker of water. The bottom of the beaker should just be touching the top of the inner cone of the flame. In the Data Table, record the time it takes for the water to start boiling rapidly. Using the beaker tongs, carefully remove the beaker and pour out the water.

11. Repeat steps 9 and 10 with the other beaker supported at a height of about 8 cm above the mouth of the barrel. **CAUTION:** *When raising the iron ring, use heat-resistant gloves.* In the Data Table, record the time it takes for the water to start boiling rapidly at this height. **Note:** *Be sure that the starting temperature of the water is the same in each trial.*

Data Table

Height Above Burner (cm)	Time to Boil (min)
2	
8	

Analysis and Conclusions

1. **Inferring** What would happen if the air intake openings were made very small?

_____

_____

2. **Drawing Conclusions** If the burner does not light after the gas outlet valve is opened, what might be wrong?

_____

3. **Observing** At what height, 2 cm or 8 cm, did the water come to a rapid boil faster?

_____

4. **Drawing Conclusions** Why is it necessary to know how to adjust the flow rates of the air and gas when using a Bunsen burner?

_____

_____

_____

5. **Controlling Variables** Why is it important to make sure that the volume of water and the starting temperature are the same in each trial?

_____

_____

Going Further

Test the ability of different kinds of laboratory burners, such as a hot plate, to heat water to boiling. Determine if there is a difference in the efficiency with which different burners are able to heat objects.

Laboratory Skills 7

Preparing Laboratory Solutions

Introduction

A solution is a type of mixture in which one substance dissolves in another. In a solution, the substance that is dissolved is called the solute. The substance that does the dissolving is called the solvent. The most common solvent is water. Most solutions cannot easily be separated by simple physical means such as filtering.

Solutions in which water is the solvent, or aqueous solutions, are important to all types of living organisms. Marine microorganisms spend their entire lives in the ocean, an aqueous solution of water, salt, and other substances. Most of the nutrients needed by plants are in aqueous solution in moist soil. Plasma, the liquid part of the blood, is an aqueous solution containing dissolved nutrients and gases.

In this investigation, you will learn some of the techniques used to prepare laboratory solutions. You will also learn some of the proper uses of a triple-beam balance and a filtering apparatus.

Problem

What are some of the different ways in which laboratory solutions can be prepared?

Pre-Lab Discussion

Read the entire investigation. Then, work with a partner to answer the following questions.

1. What does the percentage concentration of a solution mean?

   _____

   _____

2. What is the difference between the mass/volume concentration of a solution and its volume/volume concentration?

   _____

   _____

3. Why is it difficult to dilute a solution accurately?

   _____

4. What is the relationship between a 30% sodium chloride solution and a 3% sodium chloride solution in terms of the number of solute molecules in each solution?

   _____

   _____

5. Why is a chemical placed on a piece of weighing paper instead of directly on the pan of a balance when its mass is being measured?

   _____

   _____

Materials *(per group)*

sodium chloride
10 mL of red food coloring
100-mL graduated cylinder
filter paper
funnel
2 100-mL beakers

weighing paper
triple-beam balance
scoop
10-mL graduated cylinder
ring stand
iron ring

Safety 🥽 🧤 🧪

Put on a laboratory apron if one is available. Put on safety goggles. Handle all glassware carefully. Always use special caution when working with laboratory chemicals, as they may irritate the skin or cause staining of the skin or clothing. Never touch or taste any chemical unless instructed to do so. Note all safety alert symbols next to the steps in the Procedure and review the meanings of each symbol by referring to Safety Symbols on page 8.

Procedure

Part A. Preparing the Mass/Volume Solution

1. To prepare a solution of a given percentage, dissolve the number of grams of solid solute equal to the percentage in enough water to make 100 mL of the solution. To prepare a 5% sodium chloride solution, place a piece of weighing paper on the pan of the triple-beam balance and find its mass.

2. Add exactly 5 g to the value of the mass of the weighing paper and move the riders of the balance to this number.

3. Using the scoop, add a small amount of sodium chloride at a time to the paper on the balance until the pointer rests on zero.

4. Add the 5 grams of sodium chloride to the 100-mL graduated cylinder.

5. Add enough water to bring the volume of the solution to 100 mL. What happens to the sodium chloride crystals?

_____

6. Dispose of this solution according to your teacher's instructions.

Part B. Preparing a Volume/Volume Solution

1. To prepare a solution of a given percentage, dissolve the number of milliliters of liquid solute equal to the percentage in enough solvent to make 100 mL of the solution. To prepare a 10% colored water solution, measure 10 mL of red food coloring in the 10-mL graduated cylinder and pour it into the large graduated cylinder. **CAUTION:** *Use caution with red food coloring to avoid staining your hands or clothing.*

2. Add enough water to the large graduated cylinder to bring the volume to 100 mL. What happens to the red food coloring as water is mixed with it?

_____

3. Keep this solution for use in Part C of this investigation.

Part C. Reducing the Concentration of a Solution

1. To reduce the concentration of a solution, pour the number of milliliters of the existing solution that is equal to the percentage of the new concentration into a graduated cylinder. Add enough solvent to bring the volume in milliliters to an amount equal to the percentage of the original solution. To reduce a 10% colored water solution to a 1% solution, pour the 10% colored water solution you prepared in Part B into a 100-mL beaker.

2. Measure 1 mL of the 10% solution in the 10-mL graduated cylinder.

3. Add enough water to the graduated cylinder to bring the volume to 10 mL. What differences do you observe between the 10% and 1% solutions of colored water?

_____

4. Dispose of the 1% solution according to your teacher's instructions. Keep the 10% solution for use in Part D of this investigation.

Part D. Filtering

1. Prepare a filter paper as shown in Figure 1. Fold a circle of filter paper across the middle. Fold the resulting half-circle to form a quarter-circle. Open the folded paper into a cone, leaving the triple layer on one side and a single layer on the other.

2. Support a funnel as shown in Figure 2. Place the cone of the filter paper in the funnel and wet the paper so that it adheres smoothly to the walls of the funnel. Set a clean beaker beneath the funnel in such a way that the stem of the funnel touches the side of the beaker.

3. Pour the 10% colored water solution prepared in Part B slowly into the funnel. Do not let the mixture overflow the filter paper. As the mixture filters through the filter paper, record your observations in the Data Table.

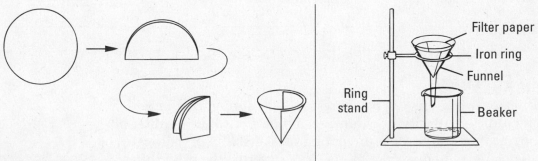

Figure 1   **Figure 2**

4. After all of the solution has passed through the filter paper into the beaker, observe the appearance of the filter paper. Record your observations in the Data Table.

5. Carefully remove the filter paper from the funnel and dispose of it and the colored water solution according to your teacher's instructions.

Data Table

Appearance of Liquid Before Filtering	Appearance of Liquid After Filtering	Appearance of Filter Paper After Filtering

Analysis and Conclusions

1. **Comparing and Contrasting** Relate the colors of the 10% and 1% colored water solutions to the number of solute molecules each solution contains.

_____

_____

2. **Observing** Was the filter paper successful in separating the two parts of the red food coloring solution? Use your observations to support your answer.

_____

_____

3. **Communicating Results** Describe the procedure needed to prepare a 30% sugar solution.

_____

_____

4. **Communicating Results** Describe the procedure needed to produce a 20% liquid bleach solution.

_____

_____

5. **Communicating Results** Describe the procedure needed to reduce an 80% starch solution to a 20% solution.

_____

_____

Going Further

Solution concentrations can be expressed in a number of different ways, including molarity (the number of moles of solute per liter of solution) and molality (the number of moles of solute per kilogram of solvent). Using a chemistry reference text, describe the procedures used to prepare 1 molar and 1 molal concentrations.

Laboratory Skills 8

Using Graphing Skills

Introduction

Recorded data can be plotted on a graph. A graph is a pictorial representation of information recorded in a data table. It is used to show a relationship between two or more different factors. Two common types of graphs are line graphs and bar graphs.

In this investigation, you will interpret and construct a bar graph and a line graph.

Problem

How do you correctly interpret and construct a line graph and a bar graph?

Pre-Lab Discussion

Read the entire investigation. Then, work with a partner to answer the following questions.

1. Would a line graph or a bar graph be better for showing the number of birds of each color in a population?

_____

2. How could you plot more than one responding variable on a line graph?

_____

3. Where do you place the manipulated variable on a line graph?

_____

4. Which type of graph would you use to show comparisons? Explain your reason

_____

5. Why is it important to have all parts of a graph clearly labeled and drawn?

_____

Procedure

Part A. Interpreting Graphs

1. The type of graph that best shows the relationship between two variables is the line graph. A line graph has one or more lines connecting a series of points. See Figure 1. Along the horizontal axis, or x-axis, you will find the manipulated variable in the experiment. Along the vertical axis or y-axis, you will find the responding variable.

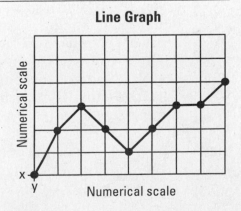

Figure 1

2. Use the line graph in Figure 2 to answer questions a through f below.

   a. Which plant grew the tallest? _____

   b. How many plants grew to be at least 6 cm tall? _____

   c. Which plant grew the fastest in the first five days? _____

   d. Which line represents plant 2? _____

   e. After 10 days, how much had plant 3 grown? _____

   f. How long did it take for plant 1 to grow 6 cm? _____

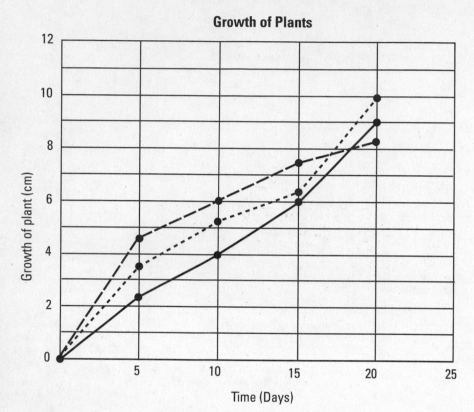

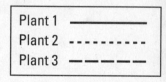

Figure 2

3. A bar graph is another way of showing relationships between variables. A bar graph also contains an x-axis and a y-axis. But instead of points, a bar graph uses a series of columns to display data. See Figure 3. On some bar graphs, the x-axis has labels rather than a numerical scale. This type of bar graph is used only to show comparisons.

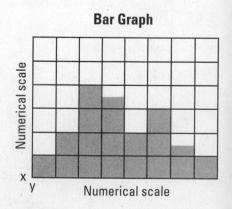

Figure 3

4. Use the bar graph in Figure 4 to answer questions a through e below.

   a. At birth, what is the average number of red blood cells per mm³ of blood?

_____

   b. What appears to happen to the number of red blood cells between birth and 2 months?

_____

   c. What happens to the number of red blood cells between the ages of 6 and 8 years?

_____

   d. Between what ages is a human likely to have 4.6 million red blood cells?

_____

   e. After 14 years of age, do males or females have a higher red blood cell count?

_____

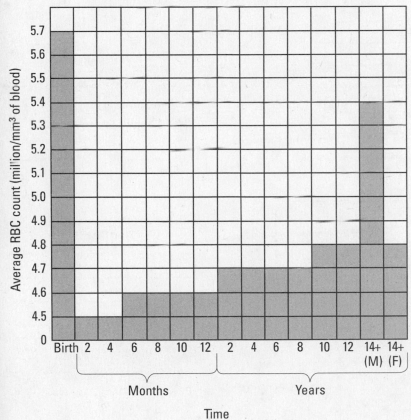

Red Blood Cell Count During Human Growth

Figure 4

Part B. Constructing Graphs

1. When plotting data on a graph, you must decide which variable to place along the x-axis and which variable to place along the y-axis. Label the axes of your graph accordingly. Then you must decide on the scale of each axis; that is, how much each unit along the axis represents. Scales should be chosen to make the graph as large as possible within the limits of the paper and still include the largest item of data. If the scale unit is too large, your graph will be cramped into a small area and will be hard to read and interpret. If the scale unit is too small, the graph will run off the paper. Scale units should also be selected for ease of locating points on the graph. Multiples of 1, 2, 5, or 10 are easiest to work with.

2. Use the information recorded in Data Table 1 to construct a line graph on the grid provided below. You should label each axis, mark an appropriate scale on each axis, plot the data, connect the points, and give your graph a title.

Data Table 1

Temperature (°C)	Breathing Rate (per minute)
10	15
15	25
18	30
20	38
23	60
25	57
27	25

Breathing Rate of the Freshwater Sunfish

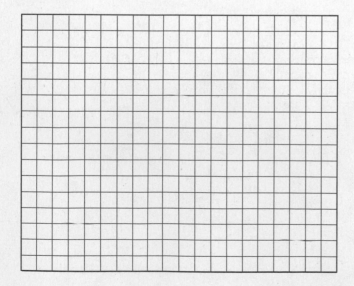

3. Use the information recorded in Data Table 2 to construct a bar graph on the grid provided below. You should label each axis, mark an appropriate scale on each axis, plot the data, darken the columns of the graph, and give your graph a title.

Data Table 2

Month	Jan.	Feb.	Mar.	April	May	June	July	Aug.	Sept.	Oct.	Nov.	Dec.
Rainfall (mL)	15	21	28	24	16	8	2	1	2	3	5	10

Average Rainfall in Willamette Valley

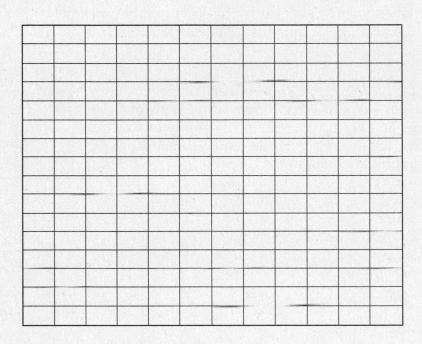

Analysis and Conclusions

1. **Comparing and Contrasting** How is a graph similar to a data table?

_____

_____

2. **Comparing and Contrasting** How is a line graph different from a bar graph?

_____

_____

3. **Using Graphs** Does a steep curve on a line graph indicate a rapid or slow rate of change?

_____

4. **Using Graphs** You are conducting an experiment to measure the gain in mass of a young mouse over a ten-week period. In constructing a graph to represent your data, which variable should you place along the x-axis and which variable should you place along the y-axis? Explain your answer.

_____

_____

_____

5. **Using Graphs** What is an advantage of using multiple lines in a line graph? (See Figure 2.)

_____

_____

_____

Going Further

A circle graph (sometimes called a "pie chart") is a convenient way to show the relative sizes of the parts that together form a whole body of data. Look through magazines and newspapers to find examples of circle graphs. Construct a chart listing the similarities and differences between circle graphs, line graphs, and bar graphs.

Observing the Uncertainty of Measurements

Introduction

Scientists use a wide variety of tools to make precise measurements. Some of the tools include a balance that measures mass in grams, a ruler or meterstick that measures length in centimeters, and a graduated cylinder that measures volume in milliliters. The accuracy of a measurement depends on three things: the accuracy of the measuring instrument, the ability of the observer to read the scale properly, and the degree of precision of the measuring instrument. In this investigation you will practice the skill of making accurate measurements using a variety of measuring instruments.

Problem

Are there differences between measurements made by two different observers?

Pre-Lab Discussion

Read the entire investigation. Then, work with a partner to answer the following questions.

1. Why is it necessary to have a particular tool for each task?

_____

_____

2. What might be a better tool for measuring the size of your classroom?

_____

_____

3. What is an advantage of using metric tools over a yardstick or ruler?

_____

_____

_____

4. Is it necessary for the same person in a group to make each measurement?

_____

_____

5. Would you expect every group's measurement of the temperature of the ice water to be the same?

_____

_____

_____

Materials *(per station)*

Station 1: meterstick

Station 2: meterstick

Station 3: 30-cm ruler
　　　　　regular object

Station 4: 100-mL graduated cylinder
　　　　　150-mL beaker of colored liquid

Station 5: triple-beam balance
　　　　　small pebble

Station 6: 100-mL graduated cylinder
　　　　　150-mL beaker of water
　　　　　irregular object

Station 7: Celsius thermometer
　　　　　250-mL beaker of ice and water
　　　　　paper towel

Safety

Put on a laboratory apron if one is available. Put on safety goggles. Handle glassware and thermometers carefully. Note all safety alert symbols next to the numbered steps in the Procedure and review the meaning of each symbol by referring to Safety Symbols on page 8.

Procedure

1. **Station 1:** Use the meterstick to measure the length and width of your science classroom. If the room has an irregular shape, measure the longest width and the longest length. Express your measurements to the nearest tenth of a meter and record them in the Data Table.

2. **Station 2:** Use the meterstick to measure the length and width of your desk or lab table. If the table has an irregular shape, measure the longest width and the longest length. Express your measurements to the nearest tenth of a centimeter and record them in the Data Table.

3. **Station 3:** Use the metric ruler to find the volume of the regular object. Volume is found by multiplying the length times the width times the height of the object. Express the volume in cubic centimeters (cm^3) and record it in the Data Table.

4. **Station 4:** Use the graduated cylinder to find the volume of the colored liquid in the beaker. **CAUTION:** *Be careful to avoid breakage when working with glassware.* Remember to always read a graduated cylinder at the bottom curve of the meniscus. Pour the liquid back into the beaker. Express your measurement in milliliters and record it in the Data Table.

5. Station 5: Make certain that the riders on the triple-beam balance are moved all the way to the left and that the pointer rests on zero. Place the pebble on the pan on the triple-beam balance. Move the riders until the pointer is at zero. Express your measurement to the nearest tenth of a gram and record it in the Data Table. Remove the pebble and return all riders to the far left of the balance.

6. Station 6: Fill the graduated cylinder half full with water from the beaker. Find the volume of the irregular object. Express the volume of the object in cubic centimeters (cm^3) and record it in the Data Table. Carefully remove the object from the graduated cylinder. Pour the water back into the beaker.

7. Station 7: Use the Celsius thermometer to find the temperature of the ice water. Express the temperature to the nearest 0.5°C and record it in the Data Table. Remove the thermometer and carefully dry it with a paper towel.

8. Compare your measurements from each station with those of classmates by having one member from your group record your data on the class data table your teacher provides. Make a copy of the class data table so that you can answer the questions that follow.

Data Table

Station	Object	Measurement (units)
1		
2		
3		
4		
5		
6		
7		

Analysis and Conclusions

1. **Analyzing Data** Examine the results from all the group measurements. Did the groups get exactly the same measurement results for the task at the same station?

_____

_____

2. **Inferring** Why is the graduated cylinder used instead of a ruler to measure the volume of the irregular object at Station 6?

_____

_____

3. **Drawing Conclusions** What are two important guidelines to follow in making a good set of measurements?

_____

_____

4. **Comparing and Contrasting** Examine all the data collected and determine which set of measurements showed the greatest variability. What are some possible reasons the measurements are not consistent for a particular set of measurements?

_____

_____

_____

5. **Predicting** Should the volume calculated for the block at station 3 be nearly the same as you would determine using the graduated cylinder technique at station 6?

_____

_____

Going Further

Test your prediction in question 5 by measuring the volume of the block at Station 3 by using the graduated cylinder technique at Station 6. Calculate the difference between the two measurements. How would you determine which is the more accurate?

Chapter 2 · The Chemistry of Life

Identifying Organic Compounds

Introduction

The most common organic compounds found in living organisms are lipids, carbohydrates, proteins, and nucleic acids. Common foods, which often consist of plant materials or substances derived from animals, are also combinations of these organic compounds. Simple chemical tests with substances called indicators can be conducted to determine the presence of organic compounds. A color change of an indicator is usually a positive test for the presence of an organic compound. In this investigation, you will use several indicators to test for the presence of lipids, carbohydrates, and proteins in particular foods.

Problem

What are the major types of organic compounds in some common foods?

Pre-Lab Discussion

Read the entire investigation. Then, work with a partner to answer the following questions.

1. What is an indicator? How is an indicator used to test for the presence of organic compounds in this experiment?

   _____

   _____

   _____

2. What is the purpose of using distilled water as one of your test substances?

   _____

   _____

3. What is the controlled variable in Part C?

   _____

4. What is the purpose of washing the test tubes thoroughly?

   _____

   _____

5. You have added Sudan III stain to each of the test tubes. What change indicates the presence of lipids?

   _____

   _____

Materials *(per group)*

10 test tubes
test-tube rack
test-tube holder
masking tape
Bunsen burner or hot plate
iodine solution
20 mL honey solution
20 mL egg white and water mixture
20 mL corn oil
20 mL lettuce and water mixture
20 mL gelatin and water solution
20 mL melted butter
20 mL potato and water mixture
20 mL apple juice and water mixture
20 mL distilled water
20 mL unknown substance
paper towels
600-mL beaker
brown paper bag
Sudan III stain
biuret reagent
Benedict's solution

Safety

Put on a laboratory apron if one is available. Put on safety goggles. Be careful to avoid breakage when working with glassware. Always use special caution when using any laboratory chemicals, as they may irritate the skin or cause staining of the skin or clothing. Never touch or taste any chemical unless instructed to do so. Use extreme care when working with heated equipment or materials to avoid burns. Note all safety alert symbols next to the steps in the Procedure and review the meanings of each symbol by referring to Safety Symbols on page 8.

Procedure

Part A. Testing for Lipids

 1. Obtain 9 test tubes and place them in a test tube rack. Use masking tape to make labels for each test tube. As shown in Figure 1, write the name of a different food sample (listed in Materials) on each masking-tape label. Label the ninth test tube "distilled water."

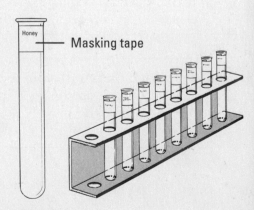

Figure 1

2. Fill each test tube with 5 mL of the substance indicated on the masking-tape label. Add 5 drops of Sudan III stain to each test tube. Sudan III stain will turn red in the presence of lipids.

3. Gently shake the contents of each test tube. **CAUTION:** *Use extreme care when handling Sudan III to avoid staining hands or clothing.* In the Data Table record any color changes and place a check mark next to those substances testing positively for lipids.

4. Wash the test tubes thoroughly.

5. For another test for lipids, divide a piece of a brown paper bag into 10 equal sections. In each section, write the name of one test substance. As shown in Figure 2.

Honey	Egg white	Corn oil	Lettuce	Gelatin
Butter	Potato	Apple juice	Distilled water	

Figure 2

6. In each section, rub a small amount of the identified food onto the brown paper. Rub the food until a "wet" spot appears on the paper. With a paper towel, rub off any excess pieces of food that may stick to the paper. Set the paper aside until the spots appear dry—about 10 to 15 minutes.

7. Hold the piece of brown paper up to a bright light or window. You will notice that some foods leave a translucent spot on the brown paper. The translucent spot indicates the presence of lipids.

Part B. Testing for Carbohydrates

1. Sugars and starches are two common types of carbohydrates. To test for starch, refill each cleaned test tube with 5 mL of the substance indicated on the masking-tape label. Add 5 drops of iodine solution to each test tube. Iodine will change color from yellow-brown to blue-black in the presence of starch.

2. Gently shake the contents of each test tube. **CAUTION:** *Use extreme caution when using iodine as it is poisonous and can also stain hands and clothing.* In the Data Table, record any color changes and place a check mark next to those substances testing positive for starch.

3. Wash the test tubes thoroughly.

 4. For a sugar test, set up a hot-water bath as shown in Figure 3. Half fill the beaker with tap water. Heat the water to a gentle boil. **CAUTION:** *Use extreme care when working with hot water. Do not let the water splash onto your hands.*

5. While the water bath is heating, fill each cleaned test tube with 5 mL of the substance indicated on the masking-tape label. Add 10 drops of Benedict's solution to each test tube. When heated, Benedict's solution will change color from blue to green, yellow, orange, or red in the presence of a simple sugar, or monosaccharide.

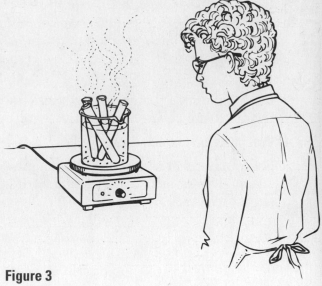

Figure 3

6. Gently shake the contents of each test tube. **CAUTION:** *Use extreme caution when using Benedict's solution to avoid staining hands or clothing.*

7. Place the test tubes in the hot-water bath. Heat the test tubes for 3 to 5 minutes. With the test tube holder, remove the test tubes from the hot-water bath and place them back in the test tube rack. **CAUTION:** *Never touch hot test tubes with your bare hands. Always use a test tube holder to handle hot test tubes.* In the Data Table, record any color changes and place a check mark next to any substances that test positive for a simple sugar.

8. After they have cooled, wash the test tubes thoroughly.

Part C. Testing for Proteins

 1. Put 5 mL of the appropriate substance in each labeled test tube. Add 5 drops of biuret reagent to each test tube. **CAUTION:** *Biuret reagent contains sodium hydroxide, a strong base. If you splash any reagent on yourself, wash it off immediately with water. Call your teacher for assistance.*

2. Gently shake the contents of each test tube. Biuret reagent changes color from yellow to blue-violet in the presence of protein. In the Data Table, record any changes in color and place a check mark next to any substances that test positively for protein.

3. Wash test tubes thoroughly.

Part D. Testing an Unknown Substance for Organic Compounds

1. Obtain a sample of an unknown substance from your teacher and pour it into the remaining test tube. Repeat the tests described in Parts A, B, and C of the Procedure to determine the main organic compounds in your sample. Record your results in the Data Table.

2. Wash the test tube thoroughly.

Name_____ Class_____ Date _____

Data Table

Substance	Lipid Test		Carbohydrate Test				Protein Test	
	Sudan color	Lipids present (✓)	Iodine color	Starches present (✓)	Benedict's color	Sugars present (✓)	Biuret color	Proteins present (✓)
Honey								
Egg white								
Corn oil								
Lettuce								
Gelatin								
Butter								
Potato								
Apple juice								
Distilled water								
Unknown								

Analysis and Conclusions

1. **Classifying** Which test substances contain lipids?

_____

2. **Classifying** Which test substances contain starch?

_____

3. **Classifying** Which test substances contain simple sugar?

_____

4. **Classifying** Which test substances contain protein?

_____

5. **Observing** Which test substances did not test positive for any of the organic compounds?

_____

6. **Drawing Conclusions** People with diabetes are instructed to avoid foods that are rich in carbohydrates. How could your observations in this investigation help you decide whether a food should be served to a person with diabetes?

_____

_____

_____

7. **Inferring** Your brown lunch bag has a large, translucent spot on the bottom. What explanation could you give for this occurrence?

_____

_____

_____

8. Drawing Conclusions What conclusion could you make if a positive test for any of the organic compounds occurred in the test tube containing only distilled water?

_____

_____

_____

9. Drawing Conclusions A very thin slice is removed from a peanut and treated with Sudan III stain. Then a drop of Biuret reagent is added to the peanut slice. When you examine the peanut slice under a microscope, patches of red and blue-violet are visible. What conclusions can you draw from your examination?

_____

_____

_____

Going Further

Test each food from a school lunch for the presence of lipids, starch, single sugars, and proteins. Construct a data table to summarize your findings.

Investigating Chemical Cycles in the Biosphere

Introduction

Living things need certain nutrients in order to continue living. For example, animals need oxygen, water, vitamins, and other compounds. Plants require carbon dioxide, water, and other compounds. Nutrients, such as water, oxygen, carbon, nitrogen, and phosphorous, move through the biosphere and may be used over and over again. The process by which each nutrient is recycled is called a chemical cycle. For example, during photosynthesis, carbon dioxide and water are taken in by plants. Molecules of water are split, releasing oxygen into the atmosphere. Many organisms use the oxygen in the atmosphere during cellular respiration. In this investigation, you will examine the role of carbon dioxide in four closed systems.

Problem

How does carbon dioxide cycle in the biosphere?

Pre-Lab Discussion

Read the entire investigation. Then, work with a partner to answer the following questions.

1. What are the manipulated variables in this experiment?

_____

2. What are the controlled variables in this experiment?

_____

_____

_____

_____

3. What purpose does the bromthymol blue solution serve in this experiment?

_____

_____

4. How will you know whether carbon dioxide is present in each test tube?

_____

_____

5. Predict the results of the experiment. What color do you expect the solution in each test tube to be after seven days?

_____

_____

_____

Materials *(per group)*

2 snails
4 water plant cuttings
pond water
masking tape
fluorescent plant lamp
bromthymol blue solution in dropper bottle
4 culture tubes with tops
test-tube rack

Safety

Put on a laboratory apron if one is available. Put on safety goggles. Handle all glassware carefully. Always use special caution when working with laboratory chemicals, as they may irritate the skin or cause staining of the skin or clothing. Never touch or taste any chemical unless instructed to do so. Follow your teacher's directions and all appropriate safety procedures when handling live animals. To avoid possible contact with poisonous or prickly plants, use forceps or wear gloves when collecting plant specimens. Wash your hands thoroughly after carrying out this investigation. Plant parts and their juices can irritate your eyes and skin. Use forceps or wear gloves when handling plants. Note all safety alert symbols next to the steps in the Procedure and review the meanings of each symbol by referring to Safety Symbols on page 8.

Procedure

1. Work in groups of two or four students. **CAUTION:** *Wear your safety goggles and laboratory apron. Be careful to avoid breakage when working with glassware.* Obtain four culture tubes with tops. Use the masking tape to prepare four labels as shown in Figure 1. Place one label on each culture tube.

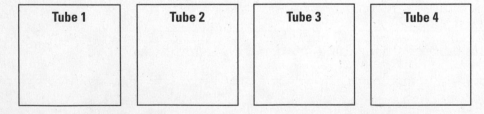

| Tube 1 | Tube 2 | Tube 3 | Tube 4 |

Figure 1

2. **CAUTION:** *Follow your teacher's directions and all safety precautions when handling plants and animals.* Into test tube 1, place two water plant cuttings and one live snail. Into tube 2, place one live snail. Into tube 3, place two water plant cuttings.

3. Fill all four tubes to the top with pond water. Add four drops of bromthymol blue solution to each tube. Seal each tube tightly. **CAUTION:** *Handle the bromthymol blue solution with care because it stains the skin and clothing.*

4. Set the tubes in a test-tube rack and place them all the same distance from a fluorescent plant lamp.

5. After 24 hours, observe the tubes. Notice if the organisms are still alive. Note any color change in the water. Bromothymol blue solution is an indicator. In the presence of carbon dioxide, it changes color from blue to yellow. Record your observations in the Data Table.

6. Observe the tubes every day for seven days. Record your observations in the Data Table.

7. Empty all the tubes and dispose of the organisms according to your teacher's directions.

Data Table

Observations				
Day	Tube 1	Tube 2	Tube 3	Tube 4
1				
2				
3				
4				
5				
6				
7				

Analysis and Conclusions

1. **Controlling Variables** What is the purpose of test tube 4?

_____

2. **Observing** What changes did you observe in the bromthymol blue solution in each test tube?
   Tube 1

   _____

   Tube 2

   _____

   Tube 3

   _____

   Tube 4

   _____

3. **Analyzing Data** At the end of seven days, what happened to the organisms in test tubes 1, 2, and 3? Explain the results you obtained.

   _____

   _____

   _____

4. **Comparing and Contrasting** Compare and contrast the events that occurred in test tubes 1 and 3.

_____

_____

_____

_____

5. **Predicting** Predict what would happen if the test tubes had all been placed in the dark for seven days. What if the test tubes were placed in the dark for many months? Explain your prediction.

_____

_____

_____

_____

6. **Drawing Conclusions** Could plants exist on Earth without animals? Could animals exist on Earth without plants? Use your data to explain your answers.

_____

_____

_____

_____

7. **Drawing Conclusions** How does this investigation demonstrate the role of carbon dioxide in chemical cycling?

_____

_____

_____

_____

Going Further

Repeat this investigation with different organisms or different combinations of organisms in each tube. You may also want to alter the size of the culture tubes or other containers. Be sure that all containers remain tightly sealed throughout the observation period. Report your observations and conclusions to the class.

Observing The Effect of Bacteria on Bean Plant Growth

Introduction

Ecologists often study the interactions of organisms in ecosystems or communities. An understanding of these interactions provides fascinating insights into the very specialized functions of particular organisms. Relationships between organisms living together can be different in nature. Parasitism benefits one organism while the other is harmed as in a tapeworm infestation of a cat or dog. In commensalism, one organism benefits and the other receives little or no benefit or harm as in a bird nesting in a tree. Mutualism differs from each of these in that both organisms benefit, as in the case of lichens (close associations of algae and fungi). Some bacteria live closely associated with other organisms. One particular type of bacterium, *Rhizobium*, invades the roots of legume-type plants and as a result, nodules or swellings develop on the roots. In this investigation, you will design and carry out a controlled experiment to determine whether the presence of *Rhizobium* affects bean plant growth.

Problem

How does the presence of *Rhizobium* bacteria affect the growth of plants?

Pre-Lab Discussion

Read the entire investigation. Then, work with a partner to answer the following questions.

1. Define the hypothesis that will be tested by your experiment.

_____

_____

_____

2. How could you test your predictions using the suggested materials?

_____

_____

_____

3. Which variables will be manipulated and which variables will be controlled?

_____

_____

_____

4. Discuss the possible outcomes of your experiment and explain the meaning of each.

_____

_____

_____

5. Suppose the control plants (those not inoculated with _Rhizobium_) developed the nodules that normally form as a result of invasion by bacteria. How could this be explained? Should this data be considered in drawing conclusions?

_____

_____

Suggested Materials _(per group)_

5-inch plastic pots (sterile)
distilled or deionized water
legume seeds
horticultural vermiculite (less dusty) or perlite
Rhizobium bacteria
plant lamps
nitrogen-free nutrients
ruler
balance (grams)
You may request additional materials if you need them.

Safety 🔬 ♨ ⚠

Always use special caution when working with laboratory chemicals, as they may irritate the skin or stain skin or clothing. Follow your teacher's directions and all appropriate safety procedures when handling microorganisms. Note all safety symbols next to the steps in Design Your Experiment and review meanings of each symbol by referring to Safety Symbols on page 8.

Design Your Experiment

    1. Prepare a written experimental design in the space below.

    Hypothesis:

_____

_____

    Manipulated variables:

_____

    Responding variables:

_____

Name_____ Class_____ Date _____

Controlled variables:

_____

Procedure:

_____

_____

_____

_____

_____

_____

_____

_____

_____

_____

_____

2. Once your teacher has approved your design, you may carry out
your experiment.

3. Record your data in the Data Table or create your own data table.
If you need more space, use additional sheets of paper.

Data Table

	With *Rhizobium*	Without *Rhizobium*	Difference	Percent Difference
Plant height (cm)				
Plant mass (g)				
Observations of roots of bean plants				

4. Calculate the difference and the percentage difference in height and
mass and record them in the data table.

Analysis and Conclusions

1. **Analyzing Data** How did the *Rhizobium* bacteria affect the growth of the bean plants?

_____

_____

_____

2. **Drawing Conclusions** Do the results support or contradict your prediction? How strongly do the results support this conclusion? Explain.

_____

_____

_____

_____

3. **Evaluating** How would you describe the type of interaction or relationship between the bacteria and the bean plant? Support your answer.

_____

_____

_____

4. **Comparing and Contrasting** Were the percentage increases for height and mass about the same? Do you think height or mass of the plant is more important?

_____

_____

_____

5. **Predicting** Imagine this experiment is criticized because height and mass are not thought to be the ultimate goal of growing bean plants. Are there any variables other than height or mass that would be better indicators of success? Are these easily measured?

_____

_____

_____

Going Further

What question(s) did the results of your experiment raise? Design an experiment that would address one such question or that would logically follow from this experiment.

Sampling a Plant Community

Introduction

A population is any group of the same species that lives in the same area. Do you know what the human population density is in the area in which you live? The density is high if the area is a crowded city filled with apartment dwellers. The density is low if the area is rural and houses are far apart.

Ecologists are sometimes asked to carry out an environmental-impact study to see how developing an area of land will affect the living things there. To do this, ecologists must know exactly what species of plants and animals there are and how many individuals are likely to be disturbed. Finding the population of many species of plants and animals is a huge task. Ecologists often take a random sampling of parts of an area and then estimate what the population is like in the larger area. In this investigation, you will use a technique called the quadrat method for estimating the plant populations that inhabit a nearby area. Recall that population density is expressed as the number of individual organisms per unit area. You also will determine the population density of a nearby plant species and calculate what plants are dominant in the area.

Problem

How can the size of large populations be estimated?

Pre-Lab Discussion

Read the entire investigation. Then, work with a partner to answer the following questions.

1. What will you observe in the 10 m × 10 m square and record in Data Table 1?

_____

2. How will you use the plant guidebooks in this investigation?

_____

_____

3. What will you do to make sure you get a random sampling of plants in the large square area?

_____

_____

_____

4. How might counting plants in three different quadrats give you a more accurate estimate of the total populations than counting plants in only one quadrat?

_____

_____

5. Using the data you will collect in Data Table 2, what two steps must you take to calculate the approximate total population of a species in the large square?

_____

_____

Materials _(per pair)_

protective work gloves

meterstick or metric tape measure

16 stakes

rubber mallet

large ball of string

scissors

plant guidebooks to woody and nonwoody plants

notepad for use in the field

right triangle (measuring tool)

Safety ✂🗑

Be careful when handling sharp instruments. Use the mallet and other tools carefully. You will be observing and handling plants outdoors. Alert your teacher in advance to any allergies you may have. To avoid possible contact with poisonous or prickly plants, wear work gloves. Use the plant guidebooks to identify dangerous plants. Do not disturb the nests of any animals you may encounter. Treat living organisms with respect. Return or dispose of all materials according to the instructions of your teacher. Note all safety symbols next to the numbered steps in the Procedure and review the meaning of each symbol by referring to Safety Symbols on page 8.

Procedure

1. Work with a partner. As shown in Figure 1, use a tape measure or meter stick to measure off a square 10 m on a side. Then use the mallet to drive a stake into each of the four corners of the square. **CAUTION:** _Be careful not to injure yourself when using the mallet and stakes._

✂ 2. Loop the string around the stakes to mark off the square. Cut the string and tie the ends together. **CAUTION:** _Be careful when handling sharp tools._

🗑 3. Take a survey of the kinds of plants you observe within the square. Use the categories shown in Data Table 1. Use plant guidebooks or other references to help you find the names of the species you observe. Write your observations in Data Table 1. **CAUTION:** _Be aware of any poisonous or prickly plants. Be sure to wear work gloves._

4. Select an area within the site for your first small, sample area, or quadrat. Do so randomly by closing your eyes and tossing an object into the square. Around the spot where the object lands, measure off a square 1 m on a side. This square is your first quadrat.

5. Use string and stakes to mark off the boundaries of the quadrat as shown in Figure 2. The right-triangle tool will help you make the corners square.

6. Observe the plants in your quadrat as shown in Figure 3. Record in Data Table 2 the number of plants in each species. Large plants can be counted individually. If you are counting grass or ground cover, measure off several smaller squares 10 cm × 10 cm. Count the number of individual plants in each of the several smaller squares, take an average figure per small square, and multiply by 100 to get an estimate for the full quadrat.

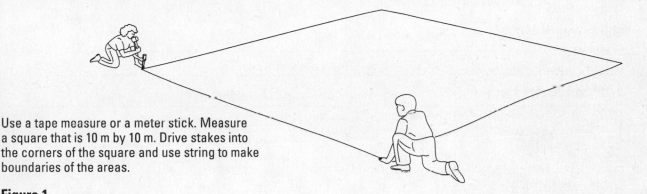

Use a tape measure or a meter stick. Measure
a square that is 10 m by 10 m. Drive stakes into
the corners of the square and use string to make
boundaries of the areas.

Figure 1

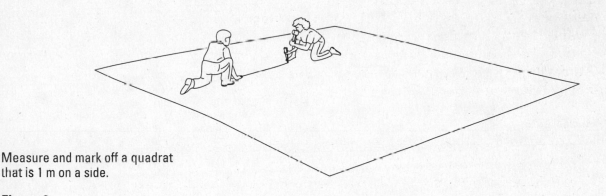

Measure and mark off a quadrat
that is 1 m on a side.

Figure 2

Use plant guidebooks to identify the plants in the square.

Figure 3

7. Repeat steps 4 through 6 twice more, to obtain population data for two more quadrats within the large square area.

8. When you have finished counting and identifying the plants, pull up the stakes, rewind the string, and return to class.

9. You now have a complete list of plant species and the number counted in each of three quadrats that are 1 m^2 in area. Average the numbers for each species by adding them and then dividing the total number by 3. This number is the species population density per square meter.

10. Estimate the approximate total population of each species by multiplying the average quadrat population by 100. Record these values in Data Table 2.

Data Table 1

Survey of Plant Types	
Plant category	**Species of plants**
Trees (including saplings)	
Shrubs (bushlike plants 0.5 to 3 m tall)	
Herbaceous plants (weeds, grasses, small flowering plants)	
Ground cover (mosses, lichens, and so on)	

Name_____ Class_____ Date _____

Data Table 2

		Populations in Quadrats			
Type of plant	**Species name**	**Number in quadrat 1**	**Number in quadrat 2**	**Number in quadrat 3**	**Calculated total population in entire area, 10 m × 10 m**

Analysis and Conclusions

1. **Analyzing Data** Interpret your data to determine the relative populations of plants in your 10 m × 10 m square. Are there mostly trees, shrubs, or herbaceous plants? What is the dominant species?

_____

_____

2. **Comparing and Contrasting** Compare your results with other student teams in the class. Why were the population densities of the various species different from one part of the overall site to another? Comment on how abiotic factors such as sunlight, terrain, and availability of water may have had an effect.

_____

_____

_____

3. **Inferring** Infer whether you would expect to see the plants in the same density 1 month, 6 months, or 1 year from now. Explain what the conditions may be like in all three cases.

_____

_____

_____

_____

_____

4. **Formulating Hypotheses** Hypothesize about how your large square area might change if human activity or disease destroyed the dominant species.

_____

_____

5. **Drawing Conclusions** Based on the results of this investigation, do you think that counting random samples is an accurate method for counting a large population? Explain your answer.

_____

_____

_____

_____

Going Further

Based on the results of this investigation, develop a hypothesis about how the average population density of one kind of plant you sampled was affected by an abiotic factor such as water or light. Propose an experiment to test your hypothesis. If the necessary resources are available and you have your teacher's permission, perform the experiment.

Investigating Air and Water Pollution

Introduction

Although life on Earth depends on air and water, we are endangering these important resources by polluting them with harmful substances. The air we breathe contains the oxygen our cells need, but it also contains many other chemicals that can damage our bodies. Our atmosphere is polluted with smog, acid rain, carbon dioxide, and a variety of other chemicals that create problems for all organisms dependent on the atmosphere.

Despite the fact that the Earth's surface is 75 percent water, only a small fraction of that water can be used by living things. The pollution of our freshwater supply by chemicals, sewage, oil, and heated waste water interferes with many food chains. It also requires costly treatments to ensure the safety of our water supply. In this investigation, you will conduct tests to determine the types of pollutants present in samples of air and water taken from the area in which you live.

Problem

How can air and water pollution be detected?

Pre-Lab Discussion

Read the entire investigation. Then, work with a partner to answer the following questions.

1. How will you choose a location to test for air pollution?

_____

_____

_____

_____

2. Why are four particle traps used for each location?

_____

_____

_____

3. How will you compare the amount of air pollution at different locations?

_____

_____

_____

4. Why should you stir each water sample before testing it for pollutants?

_____

_____

5. Examine water samples A, B, and C. Which of the water samples do you think is clean and safe for human consumption? Explain your prediction.

_____

_____

Materials *(per group)*

4 microscope slides
petroleum jelly
tongue depressors
4 petri dishes
glass-marking pencil
microscope
water samples A, B, and C
3 stirring rods
pH test paper
3 test tubes with stoppers
3 dropper pipettes

Safety 🧤🦺🔪

Put on a laboratory apron if one is available. Put on safety goggles. Always use special caution when working with laboratory chemicals, as they may irritate the skin or cause staining of the skin or clothing. Never touch or taste any chemical unless instructed to do so. Always handle the microscope with extreme care. You are responsible for its proper care and use. Use caution when handling microscope slides as they can break easily and cut you. Note all safety alert symbols next to the steps in the Procedure and review the meanings of each symbol by referring to Safety Symbols on page 8.

Procedure

Part A. Air Pollution

1. Work in groups of two or four students. Obtain four glass slides, petroleum jelly, four tongue depressors, and four petri dishes. Make four particle traps by using a tongue depressor to smear the center of four glass slides with petroleum jelly. Place each particle trap in the bottom half of a petri dish. Cover each petri dish immediately. **CAUTION:** *Wear your safety goggles and laboratory apron. Handle all glassware carefully.*

2. Select one location on the school grounds for your particle traps. After obtaining your teacher's approval, place the four petri dishes containing the particle traps in the selected location. Make sure that the petri dishes are side by side.

3. Remove the lids of the petri dishes and expose the traps to the air for 20 minutes.

4. At the end of the exposure time, replace the lids. Use the glass-marking pencil to record the test location on the lid of each petri dish. Return to your classroom.

5. Carefully remove the particle trap from the first petri dish and place it on the stage of a microscope. Use the low-power objective to examine the slide. Count the number of trapped particles and record this number in Data Table 1.

6. **CAUTION:** *Do not touch or taste the particles you collect. Always handle the microscope with extreme care, and do not use it around water or with wet hands. Never use direct sunlight as the light source for the microscope.*

7. Repeat step 6 for each of the remaining particle traps.

8. Calculate the average number of particles trapped at your selected location. Record this average in Data Table 1. To find the average number, add the number of particles counted on each trap and divide by 4.

9. Report your location and the average number of particles you trapped to the class. Using class data, complete Data Table 2.

10. Clean your laboratory equipment before proceeding with Part B of the investigation.

Part B. Water Pollution

1. Obtain water samples A, B, and C and the remaining materials listed under Materials. **CAUTION:** *Do not touch or taste the water samples.*

2. Describe the appearance of the water in sample A. Record your observations in Data Table 3.

3. Hold the sample away from your face and nose. Slowly wave your hand over the top of the container and inhale gently to determine if the water has an odor. **CAUTION:** *Do not inhale the fumes of the sample directly or repeatedly.* Record your observations in Data Table 3.

4. To determine the pH of the water sample, use a clean dropper pipette to place a drop of the water sample on the pH test paper. Immediately compare the color with the chart on the pH paper container. Record the pH in Data Table 3.

5. Pour water from the sample into a test tube until it is half full. To check for the presence of detergents, place a stopper in the test tube and shake for 10 seconds. Foam on the top of the sample indicates the presence of detergents. Record your observations in Data Table 3.

6. Repeat steps 2 through 5 with water samples B and C.

Data Table 1

Particle Trap	Number of Particles
1	
2	
3	
4	
Average	

Data Table 2

Particle Trap Location	Average Number of Trapped Particles

Data Table 3

Test For:	Sample A	Sample B	Sample C
Appearance			
Odor			
pH			
Detergents			

Analysis and Conclusions

1. **Measuring** How did you measure air pollution in this investigation? What are some weaknesses in the way you measured air pollution?

_____

_____

_____

2. **Inferring** Were there any particle traps in which you did not see any particles? Can you infer that air in such a location is free of pollutants?

_____

_____

_____

3. **Analyzing Data** In which location was the greatest average number of particles trapped? What factors do you think increased the average number of particles trapped in this location?

_____

_____

_____

4. **Predicting** In what types of weather you would expect air pollution to be the worst? Explain the basis of your prediction.

_____

_____

5. **Drawing Conclusions** Do your data support your initial prediction about the water samples?

_____

_____

_____

_____

_____

6. **Evaluating** How might the air and water pollution tests used in this lab be improved?

_____

_____

_____

_____

_____

Going Further

Conduct a study of the pollution in your community. Use the air and water pollution tests from this investigation to determine air and water quality, and make a visual survey to evaluate land pollution. Report your findings on a map of the area. Be sure to identify the major landmarks; roadways; and residential, commercial, and industrial areas of your community on the map. Your map key should explain any colors or symbols you used in reporting the data.

Chapter 7   Cell Structure and Function

Observing Osmosis

Introduction

Osmosis is the diffusion of water across a semipermeable membrane, from an area of high water concentration to an area of low water concentration. Osmosis also occurs in response to changing concentrations of water-soluble solutes. Osmosis can be observed in individual cells or in collections of cells, as in multicellular organisms or their structures. In this investigation you will use a shelled egg's external membrane to demonstrate how osmosis can occur in solutions where there are changes in the concentrations of solutes.

Problem

How does solute concentration affect the movement of water across a biological membrane?

Pre-Lab Discussion

Read the entire investigation. Then, work with a partner to answer the following questions.

1. Explain the meaning of the term *water-soluble*.

_____

2. Why does the investigation ask you to blot the egg each time it is removed from a beaker?

_____

_____

3. What are some differences between the liquids used in the investigation?

_____

_____

4. What data will you record in Data Table 2?

_____

_____

5. Why do you need to record the times the egg was immersed?

_____

_____

Materials *(per pair)*

2 decalcified eggs
paper towels
weighing container
2 250-mL beakers
distilled water

syrup
marker
2 plastic spoons
balance

Safety 🔥 👤 🧤 🔬

Put on safety goggles. Put on a laboratory apron if one is available. Be careful to avoid breakage when working with glassware. Always use caution when working with laboratory chemicals, as they may irritate the skin or stain skin or clothing. Note all safety symbols next to the steps in the Procedure and review the meaning of each symbol by referring to Safety Symbols on page 8.

Procedure

🔥 **1.** Work in pairs. Wear your safety goggles and laboratory apron. You
👤   will eventually share your data with other members of the class.

   2. Obtain two decalcified eggs, provided by your teacher. Gently blot them on a paper towel and determine the mass of each, using correct procedure (use weighing paper or a container on the balance). Record the initial mass of each egg in the spaces provided in Data Tables 1 and 2.

🧤 **3.** Place one egg in a beaker. Fill this beaker with distilled water to just cover the egg. See Figure 1. In Data Table 1 record the time the egg is placed in the water. Note the appearance of the water at this time and record your observation in Data Table 3. **CAUTION:** *Be careful to avoid breaking glassware.*

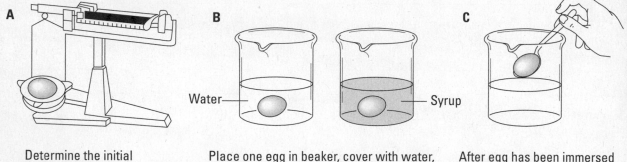

A Determine the initial mass of each egg.

B Place one egg in beaker, cover with water, and note the time. Place the other egg in second beaker, cover with syrup, and note the time.

C After egg has been immersed for 10 minutes, remove it from beaker with a spoon and set it on a paper towel.

Figure 1

   4. Place the other egg in a beaker. Pour syrup into the beaker to just cover the egg. In Data Table 2 record the time the egg is placed in the syrup. Note the appearance of the syrup at this time and record your observation in Data Table 3.

5. Using the marker, label one plastic spoon *water* and the other spoon *syrup*. After 10 minutes have elapsed, use the correctly labeled plastic spoon to remove each egg from its beaker. Carefully blot the egg with a paper towel and determine the mass of the egg. See Figure 2. Record in Data Table 1 the mass of the egg that was immersed in water. Record in Data Table 2 the mass of the egg that was immersed in syrup. Gently return each egg to its appropriate beaker. Note the times again.

A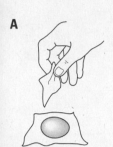

B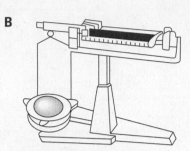

C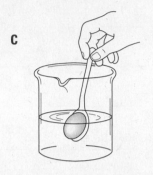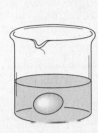

Carefully blot the egg dry.

Determine the mass of the egg.

Carefully return the egg to its beaker and note the time. Then remove the second egg, blot dry, determine its mass, and return the second egg to the beaker of syrup. Continue the immersion and weighing process until the lab period ends.

Figure 2

6. Repeat step 5 every 10 minutes, as long as time permits. Record the masses of the eggs for each 10-minute interval in Data Table 1 or Data Table 2.

7. After you have completed the last mass determination of the eggs in water and syrup, record the appearance of the water and syrup in Data Table 3. **CAUTION:** *Wash your hands thoroughly after carrying out this lab.*

8. Determine the percent change in mass of each egg for each 10-minute interval by using the following formula:

$$\frac{(\text{mass after immersion} - \text{initial mass}) \times 100}{\text{initial mass}}$$

Record this percent mass change in Data Tables 1 and 2.

Data Table 1: Egg in Distilled Water

Time (minutes)	Mass (grams)	% Mass change
In _____ Out _____	Initial mass _____	
In _____ Out _____	After 10 min. _____	
In _____ Out _____	After 20 min. _____	
In _____ Out _____	After 30 min. _____	
In _____ Out _____	After 40 min. _____	
In _____ Out _____	After 50 min. _____	

Data Table 2: Egg in Syrup

Time (minutes)	Mass (grams)	% Mass change
In _____ Out _____	Initial mass _____	
In _____ Out _____	After 10 min. _____	
In _____ Out _____	After 20 min. _____	
In _____ Out _____	After 30 min. _____	
In _____ Out _____	After 40 min. _____	
In _____ Out _____	After 50 min. _____	

Data Table 3: Appearances of Liquids

	Initial	Final
Water		
Syrup		

Name_____ Class_____ Date _____

9. Graph the percent change in mass of each egg versus time using Figure 3. Use a different symbol or color for each egg.

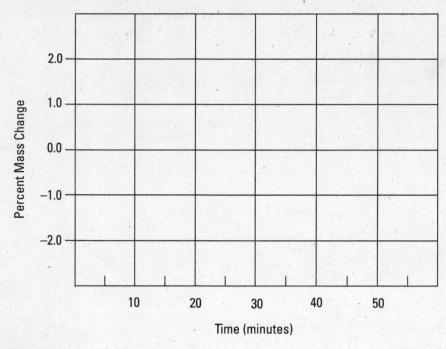

Key to symbols

• Distilled water

▲ Syrup

Figure 3

Analysis and Conclusions

1. Observing Did any egg gain mass over time? If so, which one(s)?

_____

_____

2. Observing Did any egg lose mass over time? If so, which one(s)?

_____

_____

3. Observing Describe any changes in the appearance of the water or the syrup.

_____

_____

_____

4. Inferring Explain why there were changes in the mass of the eggs, either a loss or gain.

_____

_____

_____

_____

5. **Formulating Hypotheses** Explain any changes you observed in the appearance of the water or the syrup.

_____

_____

_____

6. **Forming Operational Definitions** Using the terms isotonic, hypotonic, and hypertonic as defined in your textbook, explain the changes in mass of the two eggs.

_____

_____

_____

7. **Comparing and Contrasting** Were the results consistent throughout the class? If not, explain the sources of error that may have affected the results.

_____

_____

_____

8. **Predicting** Would you expect the same results if you used eggs that were still in their shells?

_____

_____

_____

9. **Inferring** What might you infer if the syrup's color became darker as time progressed?

_____

_____

_____

10. **Formulating Hypotheses** In the past, meat was preserved by packing it in salt. Explain how this technique might prevent the growth of microorganisms.

_____

_____

Going Further

Propose an experiment to determine the concentration of syrup or another solution that would be isotonic for an egg. If resources are available and you have the permission of your teacher, perform the experiment.

Measuring the Effect of Light Intensity on Photosynthesis

Introduction

Photosynthesis captures energy from sunlight. Plants, algae, and some bacteria use the energy captured during photosynthesis for their metabolic reactions. During photosynthesis in plants, chlorophyll and enzymes in leaves convert certain wavelengths of light into chemical energy. A simple equation can be used to represent photosynthesis.

$$\text{light energy} + CO_2 + H_2O \xrightarrow{\text{Enzymes and Chlorophyll}} \text{Carbohydrate} + O_2$$

In this investigation you will examine the relationship between the amount of light energy available and the rate of use of carbon dioxide by a plant in the process of photosynthesis.

Problem

What is the relationship between light intensity and the rate of photosynthesis?

Pre-Lab Discussion

Read the entire investigation. Then, work with a partner to answer the following questions.

1. What are the variables in this experiment? Identify the manipulated and responding variables and two controlled variables.

_____

_____

2. How will you provide carbon dioxide to the evergreen sprigs?

_____

3. How will you know whether the carbon dioxide has disappeared from the solutions in the test tubes?

_____

4. If the carbon dioxide does disappear from the solutions in the test tubes, how will you know whether it was consumed by photosynthesis or simply evaporated into the air?

_____

_____

5. How do you expect the intensity of light to affect the color of the BTB indicator? Predict the result you expect for this experiment.

_____

_____

Materials *(per group)*

8 large test tubes	dropper
4 test-tube racks	straw
250-mL beaker	4 sprigs of an evergreen (such as yew)
distilled water	paper towel
bromothymol	scalpel or single-edged razor blade
blue indicator solution	meter stick
or carbon dioxide probe	floodlight

Safety 🌀🦺🧤✂️

Use caution when working with chemicals, as they may irritate the skin or stain skin or clothing. Put on a laboratory apron if one is available and wear safety goggles. Be careful to avoid breakage when working with glassware. Be careful when handling sharp instruments. Return or dispose of all materials according to the instructions of your teacher. Note all safety symbols next to the steps in the Procedure and review the meaning of each symbol by referring to Safety Symbols on page 8.

Procedure

🌀 1. Work in groups of two or four students. **CAUTION:** *Wear your safety goggles and laboratory apron.* Obtain eight large test tubes and four test-tube racks. Place two test tubes in each test-tube rack.

🧤 2. Using a beaker, fill each of the eight test tubes with distilled water to about 4 cm from the top.

3. If you are using a carbon dioxide probe, see your teacher for instructions. Bromothymol blue indicator solution (BTB) indicates the presence of carbon dioxide by turning yellow. Add BTB to one test tube, one drop at a time, stirring with a straw. Count the drops you add. Stop when the water changes color to a pale blue. Then add the same amount of BTB to each of the other seven test tubes. Stir each test tube with a straw.

4. Using a straw, blow gently into each test tube of BTB-water solution to add carbon dioxide to the solution. Continue blowing until the color changes to a pale yellow color. **CAUTION:** *Be careful not to inhale any of the BTB solution.*

✂️ 5. Obtain four sprigs of an evergreen plant and place them on a paper towel. Using a scalpel or razor blade, carefully cut and remove about 0.5 cm from the base (blunt) end of each sprig. Cut more if necessary to ensure that all four sprigs are the same size. **CAUTION:** *Be careful when using sharp tools.* In each of the four test-tube racks, place one sprig, cut end down, into one of the two test tubes of BTB-water solution.

6. Place one test-tube rack 50 cm from the floodlight or other light source provided by your teacher. Place the second rack 40 cm from the light source, the third rack 20 cm from the light source, and the fourth rack 10 cm from the light source. Record the time you place each rack in front of the light source in the Data Table.

7. Observe the test tubes for the remainder of your lab period. Record in the Data Table the time required for a color change to occur in each test tube.

8. Compare the results in your Data Table with those of other groups in your class, according to your teacher's instructions.

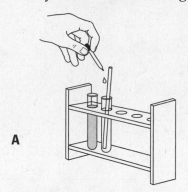

A

Add BTB solution to test tube, one drop at a time. Stir with a straw until the water changes to a pale blue.

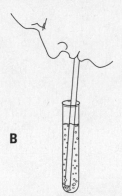

B

With a straw, blow gently into each test tube until the solution changes to a pale yellow color.

C

With a razor blade, carefully cut off about 0.5 cm from the base end of each sprig.

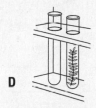

D

Place a sprig, cut end down, into one test tube in each test-tube rack.

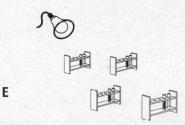

E

Place test-tube racks at specified distances from the light source. Observe any color changes and note the time.

Figure 1

Data Table

Distance from Light	Contents of Test Tube	Time Placed in Light	Time of Color Change	Elapsed Time before Change
50 cm	no plant			
50 cm	sprig of evergreen			
40 cm	no plant			
40 cm	sprig of evergreen			
20 cm	no plant			
20 cm	sprig of evergreen			
10 cm	no plant			
10 cm	sprig of evergreen			

9. Make a graph of the observations that you recorded in the Data Table. On the horizontal axis, plot distance from the light source. On the vertical axis, plot the time required for the color of the BTB solution to change. Use two different colors or symbols to graph the results from the test tubes that contained sprigs and those that did not contain sprigs.

Analysis and Conclusions

1. **Analyzing Data** In the test tubes that contained plant sprigs, how did distance from the light source affect the time required to see a color change? How can you explain this result?

_____

_____

_____

2. **Inferring** Were there any test tubes in which you did not see a color change? How can you explain this observation?

_____

_____

3. **Drawing Conclusions** Was your prediction correct? Explain what the results tell you about the effect of light intensity on photosynthesis.

_____

_____

4. **Comparing and Contrasting** Were results consistent throughout the class? If not, explain what may have affected the results.

_____

_____

5. **Predicting** Predict what would happen to the color of the BTB-water solution if you placed a tube with a plant sprig in darkness.

_____

Going Further

Based on the results of this investigation, propose a hypothesis about whether or not a temperature change in the test tubes, caused by the light source, could be a factor affecting the results. Propose an experiment to test your hypothesis about the effect of temperature on photosynthesis. If the necessary resources are available and you have your teacher's permission, perform the experiment.

Observing Respiration

Introduction
Cellular respiration occurs in all living things. During this process, animals take in oxygen and release carbon dioxide by breathing. Is it possible to observe an animal release carbon dioxide? Plants are different from animals in that they do not breathe in the same way animals do. Do they carry out cellular respiration? How could the release of carbon dioxide by plants be observed? In this investigation, you will first observe the release of carbon dioxide by humans. Then you will design and conduct an experiment to investigate whether plants also release carbon dioxide.

Problem
How can you observe the release of carbon dioxide by an animal? Do plants also release carbon dioxide as a product of cellular respiration?

Pre-Lab Discussion
Read through the entire investigation. Then, work with a partner to answer the following questions.

1. Identify the manipulated and responding variables in Part A.

_____

_____

_____

_____

2. What is an acid indicator? How and why is one being used in this experiment?

_____

_____

_____

_____

_____

3. Apply your understanding of Part A to an experiment with a plant such as a radish or bean seedling instead of a person. Why couldn't an identical experiment be used to demonstrate the release of carbon dioxide by plants?

_____

_____

_____

4. How could a new experiment be designed to demonstrate the release of carbon dioxide by a seedling?

_____

_____

5. Discuss the possible outcomes of an experiment with a seedling and explain the meaning of each.

_____

_____

Suggested Materials *(per group)*

distilled water	10 radish seedlings
hot plate	test tubes
2 500-mL beakers	stoppers
purple cabbage leaves	cotton ball
large slotted spoon	forceps
straw	

Safety 🌀🧤🧪🥽🧫🔥☠️⚠️

Put on safety goggles. Put on a laboratory apron if one is available. Be careful to avoid breakage when working with glassware. Use extreme care when working with heated equipment or materials to avoid burns. Observe proper laboratory procedures when using electrical equipment. Always use special caution when working with laboratory chemicals, as they may irritate the skin or stain skin or clothing. Never touch or taste any chemical unless instructed to do so. Note all safety alert symbols next to the steps in Design Your Experiment and review the meanings of each symbol by referring to Safety Symbols on page 8.

Design Your Experiment

Part A. Using Cabbage Indicator

1. Tear the purple cabbage leaves into small pieces. Place the cabbage pieces into one of the beakers.

2. Pour about 250 mL of distilled water into the other beaker. Using the hot plate, heat the water until it boils. **CAUTION:** *Put on safety goggles. Be careful when working with the hot plate.*

3. Pour the hot distilled water into the bowl that contains the cabbage. **CAUTION:** *Be careful when working with heated materials to avoid burns.* Allow the water to cool. The water will turn purplish-blue in color when mixed with the cabbage.

4. Using the slotted spoon, scoop out the cabbage pieces. Discard the cabbage, saving the liquid. The liquid will serve as an acid indicator. The color of the cabbage indicator will change from purplish-blue to reddish-blue when the indicator is mixed with an acid. When carbon dioxide combines with water, it forms a weak acid called carbonic acid.

5. Pour the cabbage indicator into 2 test tubes so that they are half full. Put a rubber stopper into one test tube.

6. Exhale a few times into the uncovered test tube, as shown in Figure 1. **CAUTION:** *Be sure not to inhale any of the cabbage indicator.* Observe any changes in the color of the cabbage indicator in both test tubes. Record your observations.

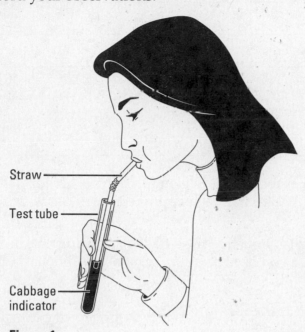

Straw

Test tube

Cabbage indicator

Figure 1

Design Your Experiment

Part B. Carbon Dioxide and Plants

1. In the space provided below, design an experiment to determine whether plants release carbon dioxide. Write your hypothesis, identify the variables, and write out the procedure in the space below. Be sure to include a control in your experimental plan.

Hypothesis:

_____

_____

Manipulated variables:

_____

_____

Responding variables:

_____

Controlled variables:

_____

Procedure:

1. _____

2. _____

3. _____

4. _____

5. _____

6. _____

7. _____

Safety Precautions:

_____

2. Submit your written experimental design to your teacher for approval. Once your design has been approved, carry out your experiment.

3. Record your data in a table such as the data table shown or create your own data table. If you need more space, attach additional paper.

Data Table

Test Tube	Description	Color of Cabbage Indicator

Analysis and Conclusions

1. **Analyzing Data** Describe the color change after exhalation into the test tube of cabbage indicator as compared to the test tube of indicator that was left alone? How can you explain what occurred?

_____

_____

_____

_____

2. Analyzing Data In the experiment that you designed, describe any color changes that occurred and provide an explanation. What happened in the "control" test tube and what does it mean?

_____

_____

_____

_____

3. Drawing Conclusions What conclusions can be drawn from the data collected in both experiments?

_____

_____

4. Designing Experiments What argument could be made against your conclusions if a control had not been used?

_____

_____

5. Predicting If the experiment is done again but more seedlings are placed in one of the test tubes, what do you predict would occur? Explain the reason for your prediction.

_____

_____

_____

6. Drawing Conclusions Did the color of the cabbage indicator change when you exhaled into the test tube? Explain your answer.

_____

_____

_____

Going Further

What question(s) did the results of your experiment raise? Design an experiment that would address one such question or that would logically follow this experiment.

Observing Specialized Cells

Introduction

The cell is the basic unit of structure and function in all living things. All of the processes necessary for life occur in cells. In single-celled organisms, all of the life functions of the organism take place within one cell. Multicellular organisms, such as humans and plants, are made up of many cells with different structures and functions. The cells of multicellular organisms take on special functions.

In this investigation, you will observe several types of cells and relate their structural differences to their functions.

Problem

How are the structures of specialized cells adapted to fit their particular functions?

Pre-Lab Discussion

Read the entire investigation. Then, work with a partner to answer the following questions.

1. What kinds of cells will you observe in this investigation? Which of these cells belong to plants? Which belong to animals?

   _____

2. In this investigation, you will prepare two wet mounts of specimens and examine three prepared slides. Why is it not practical for you to examine all of your specimens as wet mounts?

   _____

3. Why is an oak leaf probably not a good specimen for this investigation?

   _____

4. What structures do you expect to find in all five cell samples?

   _____

5. In what ways do the cells you will observe in this investigation differ from one another in function? Based on the differences in function, predict how the cells are likely to differ in structure.

   _____

   _____

Materials (per group)

microscope
lettuce leaf
water plant leaf
dropper pipette
3 microscope slides

3 coverslips
forceps
dissecting probe
prepared slides of 3 types of human tissues

Safety 🔆 ✂️ 🧤

Put on a laboratory apron if one is available. Plant parts and their juices can irritate your eyes and skin. Use forceps or wear gloves when handling plants. Handle all glassware carefully. Always handle the microscope with extreme care. You are responsible for its proper care and use. Use caution when handling microscope slides as they can break easily and cut you. Note all safety alert symbols in the Procedure and review the meaning of each symbol by referring to Safety Symbols on page 8.

Procedure

1. Obtain a microscope and place it about 10 cm from the edge of the laboratory table.
2. Carefully clean the eyepiece and the objective lenses with lens paper.
3. Locate a rib in the lettuce leaf. As shown in Figure 1, bend the lettuce leaf against the curve until it snaps.

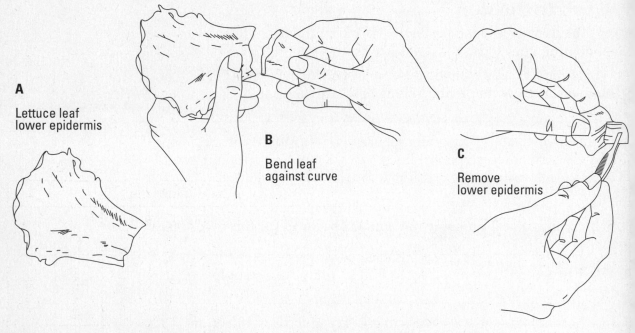

A
Lettuce leaf
lower epidermis

B
Bend leaf
against curve

C
Remove
lower epidermis

Figure 1

4. **CAUTION:** *Be careful when handling sharp instruments. Handle all glassware carefully. Use forceps or wear gloves when collecting plant specimens.* With the forceps, carefully remove the thin layer of surface tissue called the epidermis from the piece of lettuce. Spread out the epidermis as smoothly as possible on a microscope slide. **Note:** *If the epidermis becomes folded on the slide, use a dissecting probe to gently unfold and flatten it.*
5. To prepare a wet-mount slide, place a drop of water in the center of the slide. Using the dissecting probe, gently lower the coverslip onto the lettuce epidermis as shown in Figure 2.

Name_____ Class_____ Date _____

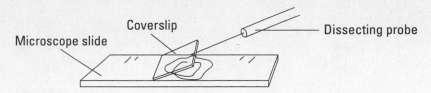

Figure 2

6. **CAUTION:** *Always handle the microscope with extreme care and do not use it around water or with wet hands. Never use direct sunlight as the light source for the microscope.* Observe the lettuce epidermis under the low-power objective of the microscope. **Note:** *It may be necessary to adjust the diaphragm so there is sufficient light passing through the cells.* Notice the shapes of the epidermal cells.

7. Switch to the high-power objective. **CAUTION:** *When turning to the high-power objective, look at the objective from the side of your microscope so that the objective lens does not hit or damage the slide.*

8. In the Data Table, write the type of cell that you examined. Describe its general shape and place a check mark in the columns below the structures that you are able to observe under the high-power objective.

9. In the space provided, draw and label what you see under the high-power objective. Record the magnification of the microscope.

10. Repeat steps 5 to 9 using the water plant leaf.

11. Repeat steps 6 to 9 using the 3 prepared slides of human cells and/or tissues.

Data Table

Cell Type	Shape	Cell Structures						
		Cell wall	Cell membrane	Nucleus	Nuclear envelope	Cytoplasm	Vacuoles	Plastids

Magnification _____

Magnification _____

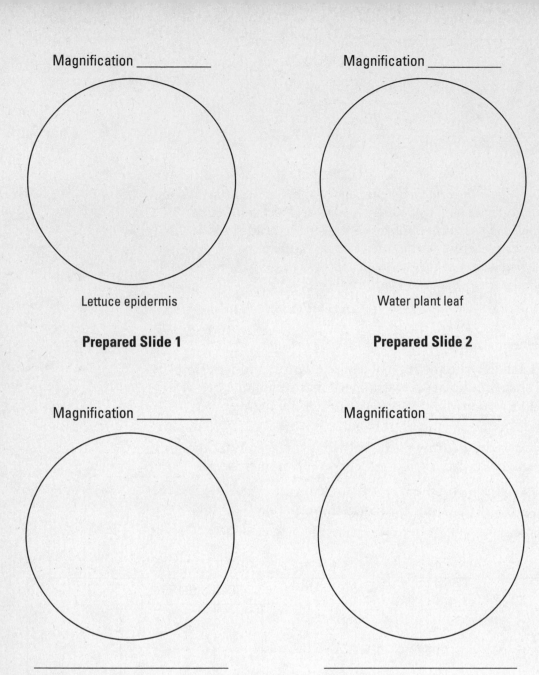

Lettuce epidermis

Water plant leaf

Prepared Slide 1

Prepared Slide 2

Magnification _____

Magnification _____

Prepared Slide 3

Magnification _____

_____

Analysis and Conclusions

1. **Evaluating and Revising** Did your observations support your initial prediction about the structures common to all the cells? List the structures all the cells you observed have in common.

   _____

   _____

2. **Comparing and Contrasting** Compare and contrast the shapes of the different cells you observed. Describe any similarities or differences.

   _____

   _____

   _____

3. **Analyzing Data** For each type of human tissue you observed, describe one feature that is not found in any of the other tissues you observed.

   _____

   _____

   _____

4. **Drawing Conclusions** How is each tissue you observed adapted to perform its function?

   _____

   _____

   _____

Going Further

Write a short report on the types of tissues found in humans and plants. Include the general characteristics and functions of each type.

Investigating Inherited Traits

Introduction

Heredity is the passing on of traits from parent to offspring. The genetic makeup of an individual is known as its genotype. The observable physical characteristics of an individual, which are the result of its genotype and its environment are known as its phenotype.

Some alleles are expressed only when the genotype is homozygous. These alleles are said to produce recessive phenotypes. Alleles that are expressed whether they are homozygous or heterozygous produce dominant phenotypes. An allele that codes for a dominant trait is represented by a capital letter, while an allele that codes for a recessive trait is represented by a lowercase letter. When some genes are heterozygous neither the dominant nor the recessive phenotype occurs. In this situation, called incomplete dominance, an intermediate phenotype is produced.

In humans, the sex of an individual is determined by the particular combination of the two sex chromosomes. Individuals who have two X chromosomes (XX) are females, whereas those who have an X and a Y chromosome (XY) are males. In this investigation, you will observe how the results of different allele combinations produce certain traits.

Problem

How are traits inherited?

Pre-Lab Discussion

Read the entire investigation. Then, work with a partner to answer the following questions.

1. What does a single side of a double-sided coin or disk represent?

_____

_____

_____

2. What is the probability, in percent, that a single coin toss will result in heads? In tails?

_____

_____

_____

3. Why is a coin toss a good way to represent allele combinations that occur in nature?

_____

_____

_____

4. For the traits explored in this lab, do all heterozygous pairs of alleles produce an intermediate phenotype?

_____

_____

5. Can you accurately determine an organism's genotype by observing its phenotype? Explain your answer.

_____

_____

_____

_____

Materials *(per group)*

3 textbooks
2 coins

Procedure

1. Place the textbooks on the laboratory table so that they form a triangular well.

2. Determine which partner will toss for the female and which will toss for the male. Remember that there are two genes per trait.

3. Have the partner who is representing the male flip a coin into the well to determine the sex of the offspring. If the coin lands heads up, the offspring is a female. If the coin lands tails up, the offspring is a male. Record the sex of the offspring in the blank at the top of page 111.

4. For all the coin tosses you will now make, heads will represent the dominant allele and tails will represent the recessive allele.

5. You and your partner should now flip your coins into the well at the same time to determine the phenotype of the first trait, the shape of the face. Note: *The coins should be flipped only once for each trait.*

6. Continue to flip the coins for each trait listed in the table in Figure 1. After each flip, record the trait of your offspring by placing a check in the appropriate box in the table.

7. Using the recorded traits, draw the facial features for your offspring in the space on page 111.

Name______________________________ Class__________________ Date _______________

Traits	Dominant (both heads)	Hybrid (one head, one tail)	Recessive (both tails)
Shape of face	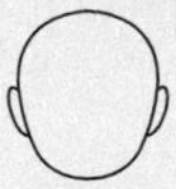 round *RR*	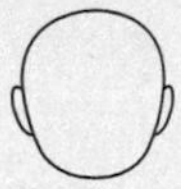 round *Rr*	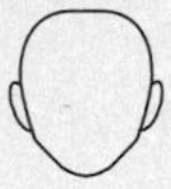 Square *rr*
Cleft in chin	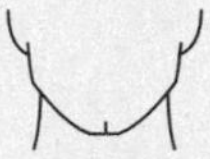 present *CC*	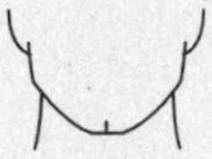 present *Cc*	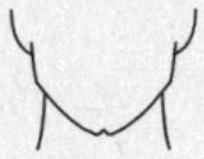 absent *cc*
Texture of hair	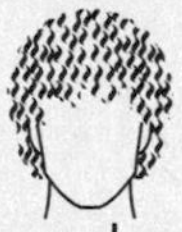 curly *HH*	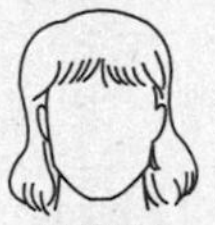 wavy *Hh*	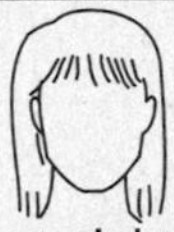 straight *hh*
Widow's peak	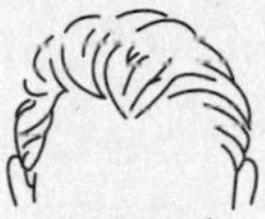 present *WW*	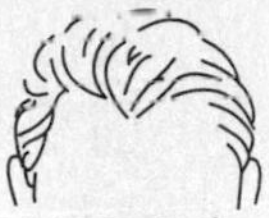 present *Ww*	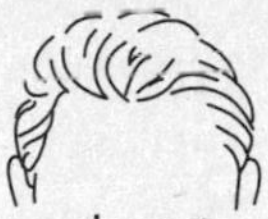 absent *ww*
Spacing of eyes	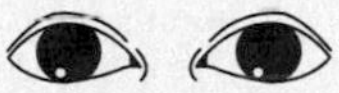 close together *EE*	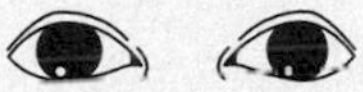 medium distance *Ee*	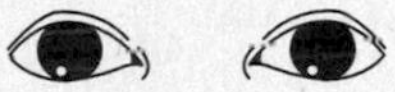 far apart *ee*
Shape of eyes	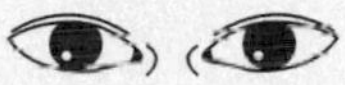 almond *AA*	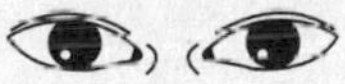 almond *Aa*	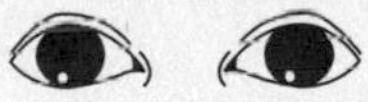 round *aa*
Position of eyes	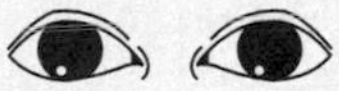 straight *SS*	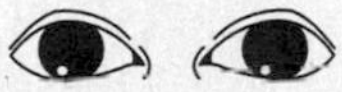 straight *Ss*	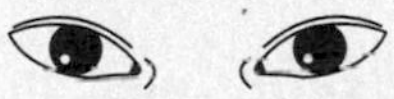 slant upward *ss*
Size of eyes	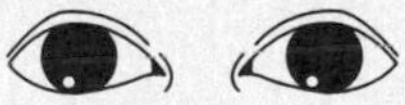 large *LL*	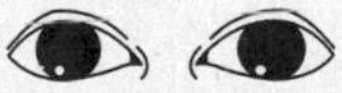 medium *Ll*	 small *ll*

Figure 1

Traits	Dominant (both heads)	Hybrid (one head, one tail)	Recessive (both tails)
Length of eyelashes	long *LL*	long *Ll*	short *ll*
Shape of eyebrows	bushy *BB*	bushy *Bb*	fine *bb*
Position of eyebrows	not connected *NN*	not connected *Nn*	connected *nn*
Size of nose	large *LL*	medium *Ll*	small *ll*
Shape of lips	thick *TT*	medium *Tt*	thin *tt*
Size of ears	large *LL*	medium *Ll*	small *ll*
Size of mouth	large *LL*	medium *Ll*	small *ll*
Freckles	present *FF*	present *Ff*	absent *ff*
Dimples	present *DD*	present *Dd*	absent *dd*

Figure 1 *continued*

Name_____ Class_____ Date _____

Sex of offspring

Drawing of Offspring

Analysis and Conclusions

1. **Inferring** What are the possible genotypes of the parents of an offspring who has wavy (*Hh*) hair?

_____

_____

2. **Predicting** Would you predict that another pair of students in your class would have an offspring genetically identical to yours? Support your answer.

_____

_____

_____

3. **Drawing Conclusions** Do you think anyone in your class has all the same genetic traits that you have? Explain your answer.

_____

_____

_____

4. **Comparing and Contrasting** How is this coin-toss model similar to the way in which traits are inherited in living things? How is the model different?

_____

_____

_____

_____

Going Further

Some inherited diseases cause an individual to die before reaching reproductive age. Using library or Internet resources, read about one of these diseases, and write a brief report about what is understood about its transmission, and in what types of populations it tends to occur. Some examples of inherited diseases that cause early death include Duchenne muscular dystrophy, Tay-Sachs disease, and Krabbe's disease.

Extracting DNA

Introduction

It was not until 1944, through an experiment with bacteria, that DNA—deoxyribonucleic acid—was found to be the carrier of genetic information within a cell. Since that time, much has been learned about the molecular structure of DNA, how it encodes and replicates information, and how that information is ultimately expressed as an organism's phenotype. In this investigation, you will use a laboratory detergent and specific laboratory techniques to extract DNA from eukaryotic cells.

Problem

What laboratory procedures can be used to extract DNA from liver cells?

Pre-Lab Discussion

Read the entire investigation. Then, work with a partner to answer the following questions.

1. After making a suspension of liver cells, you will examine a drop of this suspension under a microscope. Why will you add methylene blue stain before using the microscope?

_____

_____

2. SDS (sodium dodecylsulfate) is a laboratory detergent. What is the purpose of adding SDS to the liver cell suspension?

_____

_____

3. The liver cells in this experiment will undergo lysis, a dissolving of the cell membranes. How will you know when lysis has occurred?

_____

_____

_____

4. Near the end of this experiment you will layer ethanol on top of the liver cell/SDS mixture in order to precipitate out the DNA. Why does the ethanol float on top of the mixture? Why is it important to add the ethanol very slowly and carefully?

_____

_____

_____

5. What will you do with the liver DNA after you have extracted it?

_____

_____

Materials *(per pair)*

fresh liver (beef or pork)
scalpel or dissecting scissors
mortar and pestle
25-mL graduated cylinder
salt solution (0.9% NaCl)
cheesecloth
250-mL beaker
dropper pipette
microscope slide
methylene blue stain (0.25%)
coverslips
compound microscope
1-mL pipette with safety pipetting bulb
10% SDS solution (sodium dodecylsulfate)
95% ethanol
glass stirring rod

Safety 🧤🦺🧷✂☠🚭

Always use special caution when working with laboratory chemicals. They may irritate skin or stain skin and clothing. Put on a laboratory apron and safety goggles. Be careful to avoid breakage when working with glassware. Be careful when handling sharp instruments. Never touch or taste any laboratory chemical unless instructed to do so. Make sure that there are no flames, sparks, or open heating sources present when using ethanol. Treat all solutions containing liver cells as if they were hazardous. Return or dispose of all materials according to the instructions of your teacher. Note all safety symbols in the Procedure and review the meaning of each symbol by referring to Safety Symbols on page 8.

Procedure

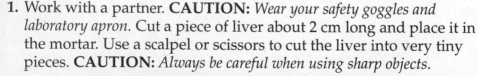

1. Work with a partner. **CAUTION:** *Wear your safety goggles and laboratory apron.* Cut a piece of liver about 2 cm long and place it in the mortar. Use a scalpel or scissors to cut the liver into very tiny pieces. **CAUTION:** *Always be careful when using sharp objects.*

2. Use a graduated cylinder to pour 10 mL of salt solution into the mortar. Use a pestle to mash the pieces of liver into the saline solution until a suspension of liver cells has been formed.

3. Fold two layers of cheesecloth in half. Use the resulting four layers to strain the liver suspension into a beaker.

4. Use a dropper pipette to remove a drop of the liver-cell suspension. Place the drop on a microscope slide.

5. Add a small drop of methylene blue stain to the cells. Add a coverslip and observe the liver cells in a microscope at both low- and high-power. Draw some liver cells and their nuclei in the space provided on page 116.

6. Use the 1-mL pipette to mix 0.5 mL of the SDS solution with the liver-cell suspension remaining in the beaker.

7. Prepare and stain a wet mount of the mixture. Make observations under high and low power. Describe the appearance of the cells in Data Table 1. Rinse your microscope slide and coverslip.

8. Repeat steps 6 and 7 approximately five times or until all the cell membranes have been broken down and no longer appear to surround the cell or the nucleus. At this point, the cells have undergone lysis. After each amount of SDS is added, observe the appearance of the cells. Record your observations in the Data Table. Then use the spaces provided on page 117 to draw cells that have undergone lysis.

9. Note the volume of liver-cell suspension/SDS mixture remaining in the beaker. Multiply this volume by 2. The result is the volume of ethanol you must add to the mixture.

A

After adding saline solution to the finely chopped liver, use a pestle to create a liver-cell suspension.

B

Strain the liver suspension through the cheesecloth.

C

Make a wet mount of the liver suspension and observe it under high- and low-power objectives.

D

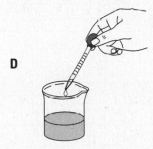

Add 0.5 mL of the SDS detergent to the liver-cell suspension to create a mixture.

E

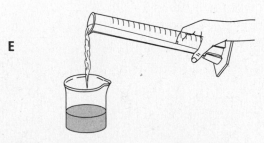

Gradually add a volume of ethanol twice the volume of the mixture in the beaker.

F

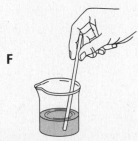

Very slowly spool the mucus-like strands of DNA onto a glass rod.

Figure 1

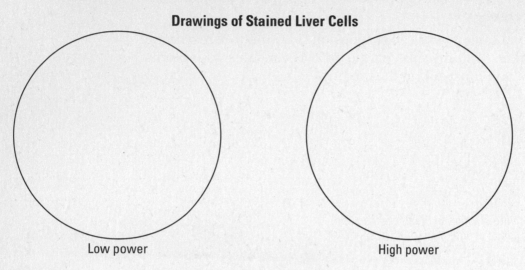

10. *Gradually* and gently pour the ethanol on top of the liver/SDS mixture. Use the glass rod to *slowly* stir the mixture. You will observe that a white substance begins to form where the two solutions meet. The substance consists of strands of DNA. Twirl the glass rod slowly in order to spool out the DNA. Describe what this substance looks like in Data Table 2. **CAUTION:** *Avoid flames when using ethanol.*

11. Prepare a wet mount of a small piece of your spooled DNA. Stain with methylene blue. In Data Table 2 and the space provided on page 117, record your description of the stained DNA and draw a picture of the stained DNA.

Drawings of Stained Liver Cells

Low power   High power

Data Table 1

Effect of SDS on Cells	
Total amount of SDS added	**Appearance of liver cells**
0.5 mL	
1.0 mL	
1.5 mL	
2.0 mL	
2.5 mL	

Drawings of Lysed Cells

Low power

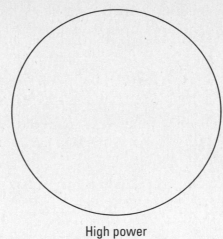

High power

Data Table 2

Observations of DNA	
Specimen	**Description**
Spooled DNA	
Stained DNA	

Drawings of Stained DNA

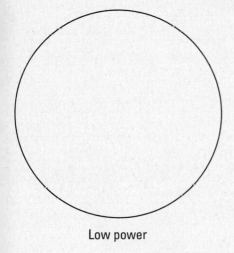

Low power

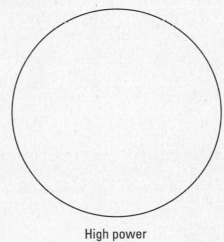

High power

Analysis and Conclusions

1. **Communicating Results** Briefly describe the steps you used in this experiment to extract DNA from liver cells.

_____

_____

_____

2. **Evaluating** Which step in the experiment did you find the most difficult? How could you make this step easier if you repeated the experiment?

_____

_____

_____

3. **Comparing and Contrasting** Compare the amount of SDS you used with others in your class. Was it the same or different? Explain your answer.

_____

_____

_____

4. **Inferring** Review the descriptions you wrote in the Data Table. How did the cells change as you added more and more SDS?

_____

_____

5. **Inferring** Why did you add SDS in a series of measured amounts?

_____

_____

_____

6. **Observing** Compare the appearance of spooled DNA with the stained DNA.

_____

_____

Going Further

Based on the results of this investigation, develop a hypothesis about whether or not the material you extracted was actually DNA. Propose an experiment to test your hypothesis. If the necessary resources are available and you have your teacher's permission, perform the experiment.

Investigating Gel Electrophoresis

Introduction

Gel electrophoresis is a method of separating molecules such as DNA and RNA by charge, size, and shape. When an electric voltage is applied to the gel, negatively charged molecules move toward the positive electrode, and positively charged molecules move toward the negative electrode. The charge, size, and shape of a particular molecule all affect the rate at which it moves through the gel.

In this investigation, you will run a gel to compare the movement of several molecules. You also will design and conduct an experiment to determine the sizes of DNA fragments in an unknown mixture using a DNA ladder (a mixture of DNA fragments of known size).

Problem

How can gel electrophoresis be used to separate a mixture of different molecules? How could this technique be used to determine the sizes of unknown molecules?

Pre-Lab Discussion

Read the entire investigation. Then, work with a partner to answer the following questions.

1. For what purposes do scientists use gel electrophoresis?

_____

2. What properties of molecules affect how they migrate (or move) through the gel? Predict what types of molecules will move closer to the negative electrode and what types will move closer to the positive electrode.

_____

_____

_____

3. The gel used in electrophoresis has microscopic pores that act like a sieve. Why would a small, compact molecule move farther through such a gel than a larger, less compact one?

_____

_____

4. In your own words, summarize the procedure for gel electrophoresis.

_____

_____

_____

5. How could gel electrophoresis be used to determine the size of DNA fragments in an unknown mixture?

Suggested Materials *(per group)*

gel electrophoresis apparatus
direct current power source
transfer pipettes
DNA samples

Safety

Put on safety goggles. Put on gloves and a laboratory apron if these are available. Observe proper laboratory procedures when using electrical equipment. Never touch or taste any chemical unless instructed to do so. Note all safety alert symbols next to the steps in Design Your Experiment and review the meanings of each symbol by referring to Safety Symbols on page 8.

Design Your Experiment

Part A. Electrophoresis Technique

1. Using a transfer pipette, carefully load each of the DNA samples into the wells in the middle of the gel in consecutive order. Load each well until it is full. **Note:** *Do not move the apparatus after samples have been loaded.* **CAUTION:** *Wear safety goggles, plastic gloves, and a laboratory apron.*

2. After loading the samples, carefully close the cover of the apparatus.

3. Insert the plug of the negative (black) wire into the negative (black) input of the power source. Insert the plug of the positive (red) wire into the positive (red) input of the power source. See Figure 1.

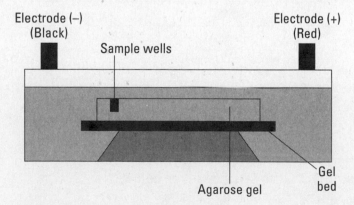

Figure 1

4. Set the power source at the voltage determined by your teacher.

5. Run the electrophoresis for the appropriate length of time based on the voltage you are using as determined by your teacher. Look for bubbles forming on the electrodes to be sure that current is flowing properly.

6. When the electrophoresis is completed, turn off the power, unplug the power source, disconnect the wires, and remove the cover from the apparatus.

7. Carefully remove the gel on its bed, holding each end of the gel to prevent it from slipping off the bed. **CAUTION:** *Make sure that power is disconnected before removing the gel.*

8. In Figure 2, indicate the relative positions of the bands of DNA.

(−)

1 2 3 4 5 6

(+)

Figure 2

Part B. Your Own Experiment

1. In the spaces that follow, design an experiment to determine the size of DNA fragments in an unknown mixture using a DNA ladder (a mixture of DNA fragments of known size).

2. Submit a written experimental design to your teacher for approval using the space below. Once your teacher has approved your design, you may carry out your experiment.

Hypothesis:

_____

_____

Manipulated variables:

_____

Responding variables:

_____

Procedure:

_____

_____

_____

_____

_____

_____

3. **Communicating Results** When you have finished running the gel, draw your results as accurately as possible on a separate sheet of paper. Number the lanes and show the relative positions of the bands. Measure and record the distance each band traveled on your drawing. Your teacher will provide you with the sizes of the DNA molecules in the ladder. Use this information to determine the sizes of the unknown DNA molecules.

Analysis and Conclusions

1. **Inferring** Why did some of the samples migrate greater distances than others?

_____

_____

_____

2. **Drawing Conclusions** How did you determine the sizes of the unknown molecules?

_____

_____

_____

3. **Predicting** How would the concentration of the gel used affect the results of electrophoresis?

_____

_____

_____

Going Further

Research a genetic engineering technique that uses gel electrophoresis such as DNA fingerprinting (for determination of genetic diseases), Recombinant DNA, or DNA sequencing. Write a short essay to explain the steps carried out in the technique and present your findings.

Making Karyotypes

Introduction

Several human genetic disorders are caused by extra, missing, or damaged chromosomes. In order to study these disorders, cells from a person are grown with a chemical that stops cell division at the metaphase stage. During metaphase, a chromosome exists as two chromatids attached at the centromere.

The cells are stained to reveal banding patterns and placed on glass slides. The chromosomes are observed under the microscope, where they are counted, checked for abnormalities, and photographed. The photograph is then enlarged, and the images of the chromosomes are individually cut out. The chromosomes are identified and arranged in homologous pairs. The arrangement of homologous pairs is called a karyotype. In this investigation, you will use a sketch of chromosomes to make a karyotype. You will also examine the karyotype to determine the presence of any chromosomal abnormalities.

Problem

How can chromosomes be observed?

Pre-Lab Discussion

Read the entire investigation. Then work with a partner to answer the following questions.

1. What clues to the presence of certain genetic disorders can be seen in a karyotype?

_____

2. Why might a laboratory worker attempting to diagnose a genetic disorder prefer to work with photographs of chromosomes rather than the chromosomes themselves?

_____

_____

3. Why would it be much more difficult to construct a karyotype of unstained chromosomes?

_____

4. Which pair of chromosomes can contain two very different chromosomes and still be considered normal? Explain your answer.

_____

_____

5. How do autosomes differ from sex chromosomes?

_____

_____

Materials *(per student)*

scissors   glue or transparent tape

Safety 🔗

Be careful when handling sharp instruments. Note all safety alert symbols next to the steps in the Procedure and review the meanings of each symbol by referring to Safety Symbols on page 8.

Procedures

Part A. Analyzing a Karyotype

1. Observe the normal human karyotype in Figure 1. Notice that the two sex chromosomes, pair number 23, do not look alike. They are different because this karyotype is of a male, and a male has an X and a Y chromosome.

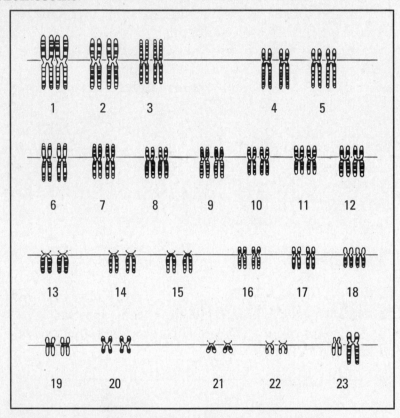

Figure 1

2. Identify the centromere in each pair of chromosomes. The centromere is the area where each chromosome narrows.

Part B. Using a Karyotype to Identify a Genetic Disorder

1. Study the human chromosomes in Figure 2 on page 125. Notice that 23 chromosomes are numbered 1 through 23.

2. To match the homologous chromosomes, look carefully at the unnumbered chromosomes. Note their overall size, the position of the centromere, and the pattern of the light and dark bands. Next to the unnumbered chromosome that is most similar to chromosome 1, write 1.

3. Repeat step 2 for chromosomes 2 through 23.

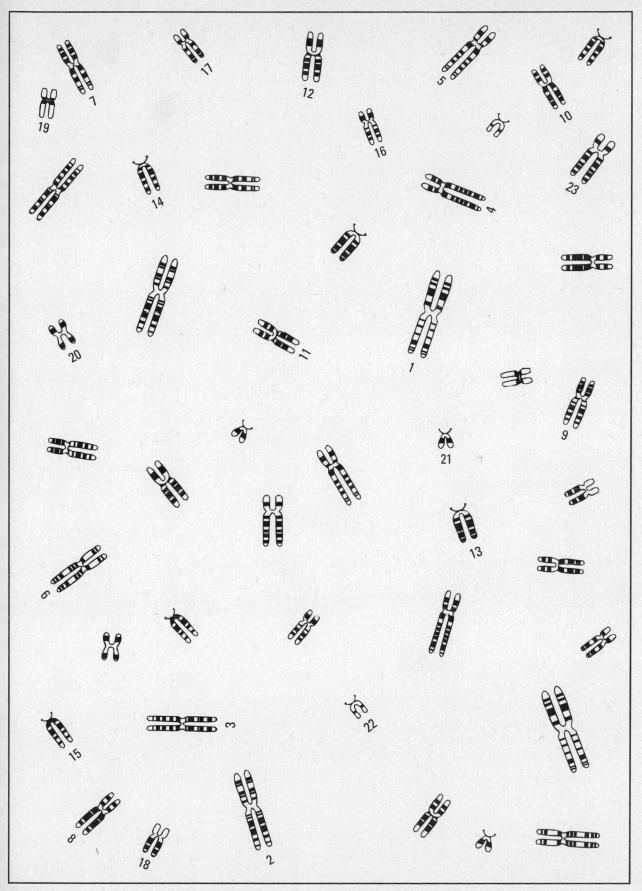

Figure 2

Name________________________ Class________________ Date ____________

4. Use scissors to cut out all the chromosomes. Tape the chromosomes in their appropriate places in Figure 3. Note any chromosomal abnormalities. **CAUTION:** *Be careful when handling sharp instruments.*

1 2 3 4 5

6 7 8 9 10 11 12

13 14 15 16 17 18

19 20 21 22 23

Figure 3

5. Observe the karyotypes in Figures 4 and 5. Note the presence of any chromosomal abnormalities.

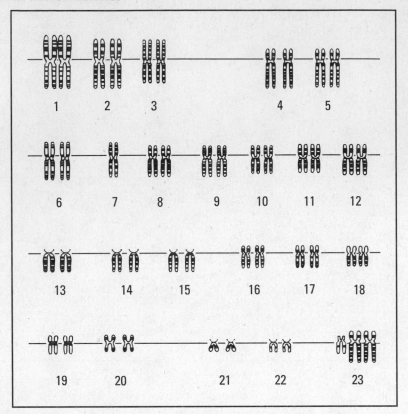

Figure 4

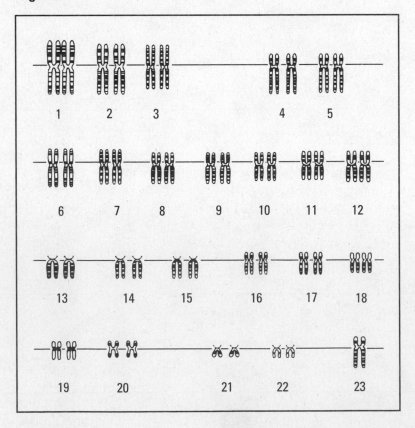

Figure 5

6. Draw a data table in the space below in which to record your observations of the karyotypes shown in Figures 1, 3, 4, and 5. Record any evidence of chromosomal abnormalities present in each karyotype. Record the genetic defect, if you know it, associated with each type of chromosomal abnormality present.

Analysis and Conclusions

1. **Comparing and Contrasting** Of the four karyotypes that you observed, which was normal? Which showed evidence of an extra chromosome? An absent chromosome?

_____

_____

2. **Formulating Hypotheses** What chromosomal abnormality appears in the karyotype in Figure 4? Can you tell from which parent this abnormality originated? Explain your answer.

_____

_____

_____

3. **Inferring** Are chromosomal abnormalities such as the ones shown confined to only certain parts of the body? Explain your answer.

_____

4. **Drawing Conclusions** Are genetic defects associated with abnormalities of autosomes or of sex chromosomes? Explain your answer.

_____

5. **Posing Questions** Formulate a question that could be answered by observing chromosomes of different species of animals.

_____

_____

Going Further

Using library materials or the Internet, research one type of deletion syndrome (a syndrome that results from loss of parts of chromosomes). Write a short paragraph describing the chromosomal abnormality involved and the characteristics of the disorder.

Comparing Adaptations of Birds

Introduction

When Charles Darwin explored the geographically isolated Galapagos Islands, he noted the great variety of beak shapes on the finches there. It was later determined that Darwin's finches made up 13 separate species. The similarities among the species suggested a common ancestor: A single species of finch that came from the mainland of South America. How and why did these birds evolve into genetically unique groups? With few native competitors and a wide variety of food sources, the newcomers were able to begin occupying niches based on variations in beak shape and size. Finches with beaks that could exploit a particular food source—insects in the bark of trees, for example—slowly secured their own niche in the new habitat. Natural selection thus favored beak specialization because it enabled many birds to adapt and coexist within the same ecosystem. Many birds also show specialization of other body parts, including legs, feet, wings, and eyes. In this investigation, you will examine the unique characteristics of many kinds of birds. What are the survival benefits of each bird's adaptations?

Problem

What adaptations have evolved among birds that enable them to survive in diverse habitats?

Pre-Lab Discussion

Read the entire investigation. Then, work with a partner to answer the following questions.

1. What can you learn from observing and comparing the physical traits of different birds?

   _____

   _____

2. What are some terms you can use to describe the size and shape of a bird's beak?

   _____

   _____

3. How does a bird's beak help you identify its habitat?

   _____

   _____

4. A certain bird ordinarily lives in or near water and spends much of its time swimming. What type of feet would you expect this bird to have?

   _____

5. Birds that spend much time perching have three front toes and one back toe. How is this different from the feet of birds that are better adapted for climbing than for perching?

_____

_____

Materials _(per group)_

specimens or illustrations of birds detailing their physical adaptations
field guides to birds

Procedure

1. Look carefully at the pictures of birds in Figure 1. Notice the details of each bird's feet and beak. Using the drawings, complete Data Table 1 by filling in one or more examples of birds that exhibit each of the beak and foot adaptations described.

2. **Predicting** In Data Table 2 on page 134 consider the adaptations of the birds listed and then predict the habitat in which you think you might find them. Check your answers using a field guide.

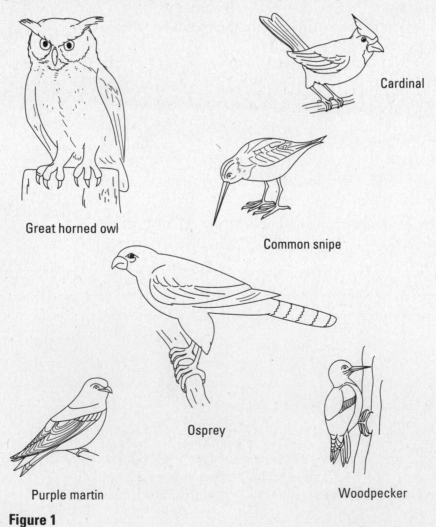

Great horned owl

Cardinal

Common snipe

Osprey

Purple martin

Woodpecker

Figure 1

Great Blue Heron

Mallard duck

Hummingbird

Pelican

Ostrich

Figure 1 *continued*

Data Table 1

Body structure	Adaption for	Type of bird
Short and stout beak	cracking seeds and nuts	
Chisel-shaped beak	breaking into tree bark for insects	
Spear-shaped beak	spearing fish	
Hooked beak	tearing animal tissue	
Pouch-like beak	holding fish	
Slender, long, slightly curved, tubular beak	probing flowers for nectar	
Long, strong, flexible beak	probing for soft-ground food	
Short, pointed, trap-like beak	catching insects in midair	
Large, forward-looking eyes	binocular and night vision for spotting prey	
Long, powerful legs	running; defense (kicking)	
2 front toes/2 back toes	holding onto side of tree without falling back	
3 front toes/1 long back toe	perching on branches	
3 front toes/1 back toe (long toes; large foot)	wading; walking on mud; walking on sand	
3 front webbed toes/1 back toe	swimming	
3 front toes/1 back toe (large, curved claws)	catching, grasping, and carrying prey over distances	

Data Table 2

Bird	Habitat
Osprey	
Great horned owl	
Woodpecker	
Purple martin	
Great blue heron	
Common snipe	
Mallard duck	
Pelican	
Cardinal	
Hummingbird	
Ostrich	

Analysis and Conclusions

1. **Comparing and Contrasting** Each pair of birds mentioned below shares some characteristics. Yet they each have their own niche; they do not compete directly for the same resources. For each pair, describe how the birds are similar and how they are different. How might their differences enable them to occupy different niches?

   a. osprey and great horned owl

   _____

   _____

   _____

   b. woodpecker and purple martin

   _____

   _____

   _____

   c. great blue heron and common snipe

   _____

   _____

   _____

2. **Inferring** Some birds, such as rails and ostriches, have lost the ability to fly. Explain how this change might have been adaptive for these birds.

   _____

   _____

   _____

3. **Inferring** Birds have hollow bones. Explain how this is adaptive.

   _____

   _____

   _____

4. **Observing** The hummingbird's beak is adapted to getting its food. Describe another adaptation of the hummingbird that enables it to get the food it needs.

   _____

   _____

   _____

5. **Inferring** Birds such as Darwin's finches are adapted to occupy highly specific niches. Would this adaptation make it easy or difficult for such birds to adapt to environmental change? Explain your answer.

   _____

   _____

   _____

6. Formulating Hypotheses Why might a bird require more than one habitat?

_____

_____

_____

7. Inferring Birds are well-adapted to their habitats, yet some birds are endangered species. Infer why certain birds are endangered.

_____

_____

_____

Going Further

Based on the results of this investigation, develop a hypothesis about the physical characteristics and habitat requirements of birds that live in hot, dry climates such as the desert. When developing a hypothesis, consider sources of food, water, shelter, nesting materials, and other factors. To test your hypothesis, with your teacher's permission, use various resources to learn about the physical characteristics and the habitat of one or more desert-dwelling birds.

Modeling a Gene Pool

Introduction

A population is a group of organisms of the same species that live together in a particular location. Each population is normally isolated from other populations of the same species. Populations can be observed for many characteristics.

Population genetics is the study of genes in a population of organisms. Biologists who study population genetics are interested in how frequently alleles of a gene appear in a population. Biologists are also interested in any changes in gene frequencies that may be occurring.

In this investigation beans will be used to represent individuals in a simulated population of organisms. Red beans will be symbols for homozygous dominant individuals *RR*. Pink (pinto) beans will be symbols for heterozygous individuals *Rr*. White beans will be symbols for homozygous recessive individuals *rr*. You will study various crosses using the beans and analyze frequencies and frequency changes as they appear in a simulated population in which a harmful phenotype occurs. In addition to this, you will be able to see how a lethal genetic disorder affects allele frequency in the population over generations.

Problem

How does gene frequency change in a population of organisms?

Pre-Lab Discussion

Read the entire investigation. Then work with a partner to answer the following questions.

1. Why are you asked to set aside and not use some of the white beans at the start of the experiment?

_____

_____

2. If the initial breeding population (the parent generation) is composed of 16 *RR* individuals, 32 *Rr* individuals, and 8 *rr* individuals, how many *R* alleles are present in the parent generation? How many *r* alleles are present in the parent generation?

_____

3. For the individuals in this lab, can the genotype of each be determined from the phenotype? Explain your answer.

_____

_____

4. Is the population represented by this lab in genetic equilibrium? Why or why not?

_____

_____

5. Predicting How would you expect the gene pool of this population to change over time?

_____

Materials _(per group)_

paper bag
red beans
pink (pinto) beans
white beans

Procedure

1. Work in pairs. Obtain an opaque container such as a paper bag. Place into it 16 red beans (RR), 32 pink beans (Rr), and 16 white beans (rr). The white beans represent a genotype (rr) that produces a potentially lethal phenotype. To represent this situation, remove half of the white beans and set them aside.

2. Mix the beans. Then, without looking into the container, remove the beans in pairs. Each pair will be one of six possible combinations, as shown in Figure 1. Count the number of pairs of each of the six combinations. These six combinations will represent the parent pairs that will produce the first generation of offspring. To help count the pairs, you may wish to divide a sheet of paper into six columns with labels. **Note:** _You will not necessarily have a pair of each type._

$RR \times RR$ $RR \times rr$ $Rr \times Rr$ $RR \times Rr$ $Rr \times rr$ $rr \times rr$

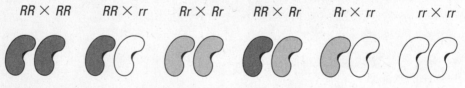

Figure 1

3. Record in Data Table 1 the number of parent pairs for each combination. See Figure 2 on page 139.

4. Assume that each pair of parents will have four offspring. Calculate the expected number of offspring for each category of parent pairs. Record these numbers in Data Table 1. For example, if you counted six $Rr \times Rr$ parent pairs, and each pair has four offspring, there will be 24 offspring for that combination. Recall from your study of genetics that the expected ratio of genotypes for the cross of two heterozygous parents is 1 RR :2 Rr : 1 rr. The expected ratio of genotypes for 24 offspring would be 6 RR : 12 Rr : 6 rr. Record the numbers that reflect your data in Data Table 1.

5. Calculate the total of each expected genotype from this first generation of offspring and record the totals in Data Table 1.

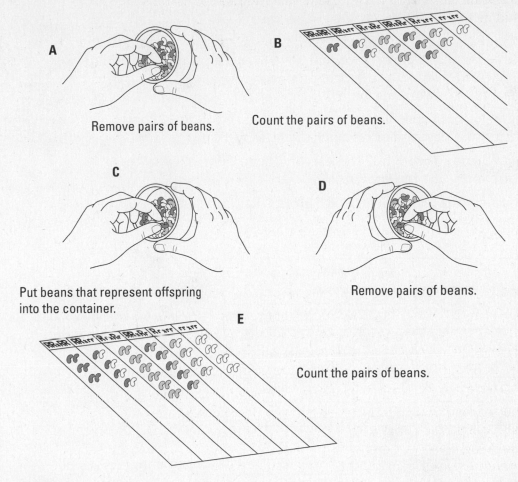

Figure 2

6. Using these totals, count the total number of *R*'s and *r*'s in the offspring population. Remember that each *RR* individual has 2 *R*'s, and each *Rr* individual has 1 *R* and 1 *r*. Record the data in Data Table 1. Then calculate the frequency of each allele by using the following formulas:

$$\text{Frequency of } R = \frac{\text{Total } R}{\text{Total } R + \text{Total } r}$$

Frequency of *r* = 1 − Frequency of *R*

Record your calculated gene frequencies in the Data Table.

7. Based on the totals in Data Table 1, put beans to represent all the first generation offspring into your container. You will need to obtain more beans since each parent pair had four offspring. As before, remove one-half of the total number of white beans (*rr* offspring) from this first generation of offspring and set them aside.

8. Mix the beans. Then, without looking into the container, pull out pairs of beans until you have removed all pairs from this new population. Arrange these pairs into the six possible combinations as you did in step 2. These six combinations will represent the parent pairs that will produce the second generation of offspring.

9. On a separate sheet of paper, draw two data tables in the same format as the Data Table below. Label them Data Table 2 and Data Table 3. Record the number of counted parent pairs in Data Table 2.

10. Assume that each parent pair will have four offspring. Calculate the expected number of offspring for each category of the parent pairs and record in Data Table 2.

11. Repeat the same calculations you did in step 6 for this second generation. Record your results in Data Table 2.

12. Repeat Steps 7 through 11 for a second generation of offspring. Record your data in Data Table 3.

13. Compare your results with other groups in your class as your teacher instructs.

Data Table 1

Parent pairs	Number of parent pairs	Number of offspring with genotypes		
		RR	Rr	rr
RR × RR				
RR × rr				
Rr × Rr				
RR × Rr				
Rr × rr				
rr × rr				
Totals:				

Total # of R's _____   Total # of r's _____

Frequency of R = _____   Frequency of r = _____

Analysis and Conclusions

1. **Calculating** Which of the six parent pairs of the first parent set (RR × RR, RR × rr, Rr × Rr, RR × Rr, Rr × rr, or rr × rr) is least likely to occur? Why is this so?

_____

_____

_____

2. **Predicting** Would you predict that another group of students in your class would have data identical to yours? Explain your answer.

_____

_____

_____

3. **Drawing Conclusions** Does every factor that affects the reproductive success of only some individuals in a population result in evolution? Explain your answer.

_____

_____

_____

4. **Using Models** Is this experiment a valid model for uncomplicated inheritance, in general, in a large population? Explain your answer.

_____

_____

_____

5. **Forming Operational Definitions** Evolution is change of a population over generations. Form an operational definition of evolution as it occurs in this model.

_____

_____

Going Further

Sometimes the relationship between a certain phenotype and overall reproductive success is not a simple one. Using library or Internet resources, research the incidence of sickle cell anemia, an inherited disorder, and its relationship to malaria, a disease due to a pathogen. Use this example to explain how natural selection can work to keep a harmful allele in a population.

Making Coacervates

Introduction

How did life on Earth begin? According to a hypothesis by Russian scientist Alexander Oparin, all life developed gradually from materials found in the oceans on primitive Earth. According to Oparin, prehistoric oceans probably consisted of a rich mixture of organic chemicals, including proteins and carbohydrates. If certain kinds of proteins and carbohydrates are mixed together with water, coacervates, or droplets showing lifelike characteristics, may form. Coacervates are not alive. However, in a manner similar to cells, coacervates appear to ingest materials, grow, and reproduce. Because of this, scientists have hypothesized that coacervates may have been among the precursors of cells. In this investigation, you will produce coacervates and observe their behavior.

Problem

How does a mixture of protein and carbohydrate molecules act like a living organism?

Pre-Lab Discussion

Read the entire investigation. Then, work with a partner to answer the following questions.

1. What mixture will you prepare at the beginning of the investigation?

   _____

2. Why does the investigation ask you to gradually increase the acidity of the mixture?

   _____

   _____

3. What will you do with the coacervates once you have made them?

   _____

   _____

4. What characteristics of living organisms do you predict coacervates will show?

   _____

5. How will this investigation help you understand scientific theories about how life on Earth first began?

   _____

   _____

   _____

Suggested Materials *(per group)*

1 medium-sized test tube
1 rubber stopper that fits the test tube
1% gelatin solution
1% gum arabic solution
1% hydrochloric acid solution
pH test paper
2 dropper pipettes
microscope
microscope slide
coverslip
10-mL graduated cylinder
glass stirring rod
water-soluble dye
oil-soluble dye

Safety

Put on a laboratory apron if one is available. Put on safety goggles. Handle all glassware carefully. Always use special caution when working with laboratory chemicals as they may irritate the skin or cause staining of the skin or clothing. Never touch or taste any chemical unless you are instructed to do so. Always handle the microscope with extreme care. You are responsible for its proper care and use. Use caution when handling microscope slides as they can break easily and cut you. Note all safety alert symbols next to the steps in Design Your Experiment and review the meaning of each symbol by referring to Safety Symbols on page 8.

Design Your Experiment

Part A. Making Coacervates

1. Obtain a test tube and a rubber stopper that fits the test tube. Use the graduated cylinder to pour 6 mL of gelatin solution into the test tube. Next add 4 mL of gum arabic solution to the test tube. Mix the two solutions by gently inverting the test tube several times. **Note:** *Mix the solutions gently. Do not shake the test tube, as this will hinder the formation of coacervates.* **CAUTION:** *Wear your safety goggles and laboratory apron.*

2. Coacervates will form only under specific environmental conditions. One important condition is the acidity of the environment. Unstopper the test tube and dip a glass stirring rod into the mixture. Touch a drop of the mixture onto a piece of pH paper. Compare the color of your pH paper to information given on the package of test papers or information supplied by your teacher. Record the pH under Trial 1 in the Data Table.

3. The cloudiness or clearness of the mixture may indicate the presence or absence of coacervates. Hold the test tube up to a light source. Record if the mixture is cloudy or clear under Trial 1 in the Data Table.

4. Use a dropper pipette to put 2 drops of the mixture on a clean microscope slide. Place a coverslip over the drops and examine them under low power. Coacervates, as shown in Figure 1, look like droplets of material with tiny bubbles inside. **Note:** *You may not see coacervates until the pH (acidity) is adjusted, so do not get discouraged.* Observe the number, size, and movement of any coacervates present and record this information under Trial 1 in the Data Table. Clean the slide and coverslip.

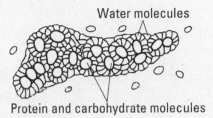

Water molecules

Protein and carbohydrate molecules

Figure 1

5. Use a second dropper pipette to change the pH of the mixture by adding 3 drops of weak hydrochloric acid solution. **CAUTION:** *Hydrochloric acid can cause burns. If the acid touches your skin or clothes, immediately wash the area with water and notify your teacher.* Stopper the test tube and gently invert it once or twice to mix the solution.

6. Repeat steps 2 through 4, recording all information under Trial 2 in the Data Table.

7. Repeat step 5 four more times, adding 3 drops of weak hydrochloric acid each time. Test the pH of the mixture, observe and record the degree of cloudiness, and make observations of coacervates under the microscope. Record this information under Trials 3 through 6 in the Data Table.

Data Table

	Observation of Coacervates					
	Trial					
	1	2	3	4	5	6
pH						
Cloudy/clear						
Microscopic observations						

Part B. Your Own Experiment

1. One characteristic of living cells is selective permeability. Now that you have determined the best pH for making coacervates, design an experiment to determine whether coacervates are equally permeable to water-soluble substances and oil-soluble substances. You can use water-soluble and oil-soluble dyes in your experiment.

2. With your teacher's approval, carry out your experiment.

Analysis and Conclusions

1. **Analyzing Data** At what pH do coacervates appear to be the largest and most abundant?

_____

2. **Analyzing Data** How does the cloudiness of the solution relate to the presence or absence of coacervates?

_____

3. **Drawing Conclusions** Did the results of your experiment support the hypothesis that coacervates are selectively permeable? Explain your answer.

_____

_____

4. **Comparing and Contrasting** How are coacervates similar to living organisms? How are they different?

_____

_____

_____

5. **Formulating Hypotheses** Do you think your coacervate investigation might have worked if you had substituted other proteins and carbohydrates? How could you test your hypothesis?

_____

_____

Going Further

Use resources in the library or on the internet to learn about Sidney Fox's experiments on proteinoid microspheres. Design an experiment to make microspheres and compare their characteristics to living cells. If the necessary resources are available and you have your teacher's permission, perform the experiment.

Using and Constructing a Classification Key

Introduction

All cultures have developed names for the living things found in their local environments. However, confusion is possible when different informal names are used for the same organism, so scientists have developed an international system for naming and classifying all organisms. Identification guides, called keys, have been developed to help us recognize and identify organisms according to their scientific names.

   Classification keys are usually dichotomous in arrangement. The word dichotomous comes from the word dichotomy meaning "two opposite parts or categories." A dichotomous key gives the reader a series of opposing descriptions of basic features of the organism. The reader studies the specimen and selects the descriptions that apply to it until reaching a statement that characterizes only one species and names it. In this investigation you will use a typical dichotomous key to identify the genus and species of several different salamanders. Then, you will create your own dichotomous key to categorize a diverse group of wildflowers.

Problem

How is a dichotomous key used to distinguish among similar organisms?

Pre-Lab Discussion

Read the entire investigation. Then, work with a partner to answer the following questions.

1. How many choices does a dichotomous key provide at each step?

_____

2. What are some of the apparent differences among the salamanders illustrated?

_____

_____

3. What is a distinguishing characteristic of the members of the genus *Ambystoma*?

_____

_____

4. What is a good strategy for beginning to create a classification key for the six types of wildflowers shown in the diagram?

_____

_____

5. If you were using live flowers, what other characteristics could you use to identify them?

_____

Procedure

Part A: Using a Classification Key

1. Examine the drawings of the salamanders in Figure 1.

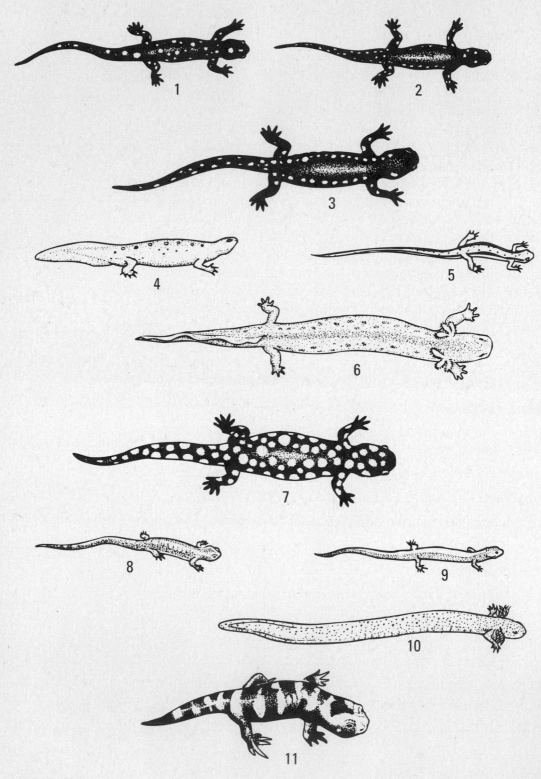

Figure 1

Name_____ Class_____ Date _____

2. Use the dichotomous key (Figure 2) to determine the genus and species of a salamander in Figure 1. Begin by reading statements 1a and 1b. One of the statements describes the salamander; the other statement does not. Follow the directions for the statement that applies to the salamander and continue following the correct statements until you have identified it. Record the scientific and common name of the salamander in the Data Table on page 150.

3. Repeat step 2 for each of the other salamanders in Figure 1.

1	a	Hind limbs absent	*Siren intermedia*, siren
	b	Hind limbs present	Go to 2
2	a	External gills present in adults	*Necturus maculosus*, mud puppy
	b	External gills absent in adults	Go to 3
3	a	Large size (over 7 cm long in Figure 1)	Go to 4
	b	Small size (under 7 cm long in Figure 1)	Go to 5
4	a	Body background black, large white spots variable in size completely covering body and tail	*Ambystoma tigrinum*, tiger salamander
	b	Body background black, small round white spots in a row along each side from eye to tip of tail	*Ambystoma maculatum*, spotted salamander
5	a	Body background black with white spots	Go to 6
	b	Body background light color with dark spots and/or lines on body	Go to 7
6	a	Small white spots on black background in a row along each side from head to tip of tail	*Ambystoma jeffersonianum*, Jefferson salamander
	b	Small white spots scattered throughout a black background from head to tip of tail	*Plethodon glutinosus*, slimy salamander
7	a	Large irregular white spots on a black background extending from head to tip of tail	*Ambystoma opacum*, marbled salamander
	b	No large irregular black spots on a light background	Go to 8
8	a	Round spots scattered along back and sides of body, tail flattened like a tadpole	*Triturus viridescens*, newt
	b	Without round spots and tail not flattened like a tadpole	Go to 9
9	a	Two dark lines bordering a broad light middorsal stripe with a narrow median dark line extending from the head onto the tail	*Eurycea bislineata*, two-lined salamander
	b	Without two dark lines running the length of the body	Go to 10
10	a	A light stripe running the length of the body and bordered by dark pigment extending downward on the sides	*Plethodon cinereus*, red-backed salamander
	b	A light stripe extending the length of the body, a marked constriction at the base of the tail	*Hemidactylium scutatum*, four-toed salamander

Figure 2

Data Table

Number	Genus and species	Common name
1		
2		
3		
4		
5		
6		
7		
8		
9		
10		
11		

Part B. Contructing a Classification Key

1. Examine Figure 3, which shows some common North American wildflowers. Note different characteristics in flower shape, number of petals, and leaf number and shape.

Figure 3

2. Use the space below to construct a dichotomous classification key for the wildflowers in Figure 3. Be sure to use enough pairs of statements to have a final positive statement for each to identify each of the six flowers shown. Use the key to salamanders as a model for developing your wildflower key.

3. Check the usefulness of your wildflower key by letting another student see if he or she can use it to identify each pictured flower.

Wildflower Classification Key

Analysis and Conclusions

1. Analyzing Data What are some examples of basic differences among the salamanders pictured?

_____

_____

2. Inferring Does the presence of external gills in some of the salamanders suggest that all salamanders may have an immature stage when they have gills like a tadpole?

_____

_____

_____

3. **Drawing Conclusions** Do the classification keys you have just worked with have any limitations in distinguishing between species?

_____

_____

4. **Comparing and Contrasting** Do any of the wildflowers shown in Figure 3 appear to be similar enough to be in the same genus?

_____

_____

5. **Evaluating** What characteristics should be very similar in order to support the prediction that two plants are closely related?

_____

_____

6. **Drawing Conclusions** Are the three salamanders from the genus *Ambystoma* more closely related than *Necturus*, the mud puppy, and *Triturus*, the newt?

_____

_____

Going Further

Construct an evolutionary tree diagram based on the physical similarities and differences of the salamanders shown in Figure 1. Assume that those most similar share a recent ancestor and those that are most different had a common ancestor long ago.

Controlling Bacterial Growth

Introduction

Chemical substances that either kill bacteria or inhibit bacterial growth are called antimicrobial agents. Antimicrobial agents are of three basic types: antiseptics, or chemicals used to inhibit the growth of or kill bacteria on living tissues; disinfectants, or chemicals used to inhibit the growth of or kill bacteria on nonliving things; and antibiotics, or chemical substances produced by living organisms, which inhibit the growth of bacteria.

The effectiveness of each type of antimicrobial agent is influenced by many factors. Some of these factors include the environmental conditions in which the agent is applied, the chemical properties of the agent, how long the agent has been stored, and the rate of deterioration of the agent.

In this investigation, you will test the effectiveness of disinfectants and antibiotics in inhibiting the growth of bacteria.

Problem

How can the growth of bacteria be controlled?

Pre-Lab Discussion

Read the entire investigation. Then, work with a partner to answer the following questions.

1. Why is it important not to open sterile agar plates?

_____

_____

2. Why do you think it is so important to write only near the edges of the petri dish?

_____

_____

3. Why is it important to use sterile techniques while inoculating the agar plates?

_____

_____

4. What is the purpose of the disk soaked in distilled water in each inoculated petri dish?

_____

_____

5. What is the purpose of taping closed the lids of the petri dishes?

_____

_____

Materials (per group)

glass-marking pencil
Bunsen burner
flint striker or matches
2 sterile cotton swabs
beaker of water
test-tube rack
sterile filter-paper disks
sterile forceps
distilled water
metric ruler
transparent tape

culture of *Escherichia coli*
2 sterile nutrient agar plates
3 disinfectants chosen from the
following: chlorine bleach,
household cleaner, household
disinfectant, phenol
3 antibiotic disks chosen from
the following: aureomycin,
chloromycetin, penicillin,
streptomycin, tetracycline,
terramycin

Safety 🗑🏠🧤💧⚗☠🔥🔲🔥

Put on safety goggles. Put on a laboratory apron if one is available.
Be careful to avoid breakage when working with glassware. Tie back
loose hair when working with flames. Do not reach over an open
flame. Always follow your teacher's directions and use special caution
when working with bacterial cultures. Wash your hands thoroughly
after carrying out this investigation. Return or dispose of all materials
according to the instructions of your teacher. Note all safety symbols
next to the steps in the Procedure and review the meaning of each
symbol by referring to Safety Symbols on page 8.

Procedure

Part A. Inoculating a Sterile Nutrient Agar Plate

1. Obtain two sterile nutrient agar plates. Carefully turn over each
plate and lay it on your worktable. **CAUTION:** *Be very careful not to
open the petri dishes of sterile agar while handling them.*

2. With a glass-marking pencil, mark the bottom of each
petri dish shown in Figure 1. Draw two lines at right
angles to each other so that the dish is divided into
four equal areas, or quadrants. Number the
quadrants on each dish 1 through 4. **Note:** *Place the
numbers near the edges of the dishes.* Write your initials
near the top center of each dish. Carefully turn the
petri dishes right side up.

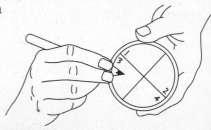

Figure 1

3. Obtain a test tube containing a bacterial culture of
Escherichia coli. Place the test tube in a test-tube rack. **CAUTION:**
*Use extreme care when working with bacterial cultures. Avoid spills. If a
spill does occur, immediately call your teacher for assistance.* Obtain two
sterile cotton swabs. Carefully read steps 4 through 8 and study
Figure 2 before you proceed.

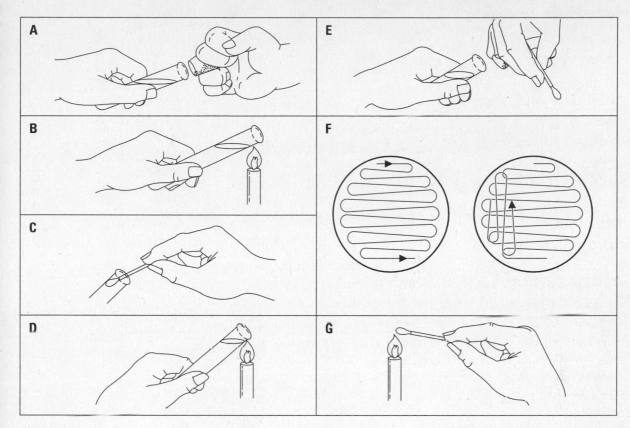

Figure 2

 4. Put on your safety goggles and light the Bunsen burner.
CAUTION: *Use extreme care when working with or near an open flame. Tie back loose hair and clothing.*

5. Pick up the test tube of *E. coli.* Remove the cotton plug. **Note:** *Do not let the cotton plug come in contact with any other object.* Pass the mouth of the tube back and forth through the burner flame.

6. Insert a sterile cotton swab into the bacterial culture. **Note:** *Shake any excess liquid into the test tube.* Remove the cotton swab. **Note:** *Do not let the cotton swab come in contact with any other object.* Pass the mouth of the tube back and forth through the burner flame. Replace the cotton plug and return the test tube to the rack.

7. Slightly open a sterile nutrient agar plate. Place the tip of the cotton swab near the top center of the agar. Streak the agar as shown in Figure 3A. Lift the swab off the plate and turn the petri dish 90° to the right. Streak the agar again, as shown in Figure 3B. Close the petri dish.

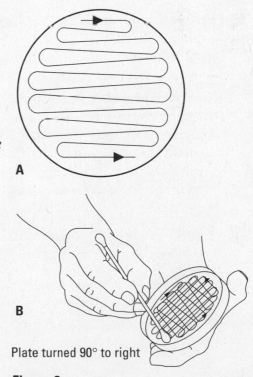

Plate turned 90° to right

Figure 3

8. Hold the top of the cotton swab in the flame of the Bunsen burner until it catches fire. Remove the swab from the flame and plunge it into a beaker of water.

9. Repeat steps 5 through 8 for the other sterile nutrient agar plate. **Note:** *Be sure to use a new sterile cotton swab for this transfer.* Turn off the Bunsen burner after you have completed the second plate.

10. The nutrient agar plates that you have just streaked, or inoculated, with bacteria will be used in Part B of this investigation.

11. Return the test tube of *E. coli* to your teacher. Thoroughly wash your hands with soap and water.

Part B. Controlling the Spread of Bacteria with Disinfectants and Antibiotics

1. Take one inoculated agar plate of *E. coli* that you prepared in Part A.

2. Select three disinfectants and three antibiotics, and record these selections in the Data Table. Carefully read steps 3 through 10 and study Figure 4 before you proceed.

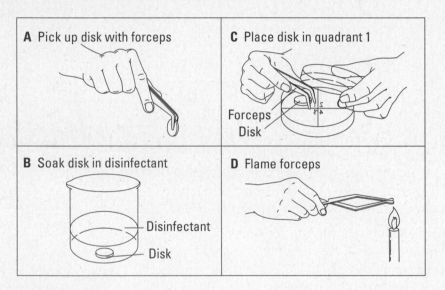

A Pick up disk with forceps

C Place disk in quadrant 1

Forceps
Disk

B Soak disk in disinfectant

Disinfectant
Disk

D Flame forceps

Figure 4

3. Light the Bunsen burner. **CAUTION:** *Use extreme care when working with or near an open flame. Tie back loose hair and clothing.*

4. With sterile forceps, pick up a disk of filter paper. Insert the disk into disinfectant 1. Shake off any excess liquid.

5. Slightly open an inoculated agar plate. Position the filter-paper disk in the center of quadrant 1. With the tip of the forceps, gently press the disk against the agar until it sticks. Remove the forceps and close the petri dish.

6. Pass the forceps back and forth through the flame of the Bunsen burner several times. This procedure sterilizes the forceps.
CAUTION: *If there is alcohol on the forceps, it will burn brightly and quickly. Stand back from the Bunsen burner when burning alcohol off the forceps.* Allow the forceps to cool before picking up the next filter-paper disk.

7. Repeat steps 4 through 6 with the remaining disinfectant-soaked disks in quadrants 2 and 3 of the inoculated plate of *E. coli*. **Note:** *Remember to sterilize the forceps after each use.*

8. In quadrant 4, place a filter-paper disk soaked in distilled water.

9. Repeat steps 4 through 8 with the other inoculated agar plate using antibiotic disks instead of disinfectants. You should have two inoculated agar plates as shown in Figure 5.

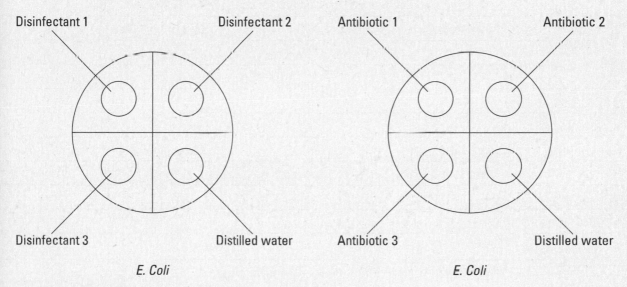

Figure 5

10. With transparent tape, tape the petri dishes closed, as shown in Figure 6. Turn the dishes upside down. Incubate the dishes for 48 hours at 37°C.

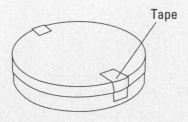

Figure 6

11. Observe the petri dishes after 48 hours. White or cloudy areas of the agar indicate bacterial growth. Notice any clear areas, called *zones of inhibition*, surrounding the filter-paper disks. A clear area indicates that the disinfectant or antibiotic inhibited bacterial growth. A lightly cloudy area surrounding a disk indicates that bacterial growth was slowed down. **Note:** *You may want to hold the petri dishes to the light to see the zones of inhibition more clearly.*

12. With a metric ruler, measure to the nearest millimeter the size of the clear zone surrounding each disk. Record your measurements in the Data Table. If no clear zone is present, record the measurement as 0.

13. Return the petri dishes to your teacher for proper disposal. Thoroughly wash your hands with soap and water.

Data Table

Effects of Disinfectants and Antibiotics on Growth of *E. Coli*	
Disinfectant	**Zone of inhibition** (mm)
1	
2	
3	
4 distilled water	
Antibiotic	**Zone of inhibition** (mm)
1	
2	
3	
4 distilled water	

Analysis and Conclusions

1. **Observing** Which disinfectant was most effective in preventing the growth of *E. coli*?

2. **Observing** Which antibiotic was most effective in preventing the growth of *E. coli*?

3. **Controlling Variables** How do you know that any inhibition you have observed is due to the disinfectants and antibiotics on the disk?

4. **Analyzing Data** Pretend that a serious staphylococcus infection has developed in the locker room of your school's gym. Assume that you are responsible for getting rid of the staph contamination. How would you do so?

5. **Formulating Hypotheses** Scientists have observed that an antibiotic seems to lose its effectiveness against a particular population of bacteria after a prolonged period of time. What do you think is responsible for this phenomenon?

_____

_____

_____

6. **Formulating Hypotheses** Why are the different disinfectants not equally effective against all species of bacteria?

_____

_____

7. **Inferring** Suppose that your doctor diagnoses your condition as a bacterial infection and prescribes an antibiotic. Your doctor cautions you to take the antibiotic for 10 days even though you may feel fine after a few days. Explain why you should follow your doctor's orders.

_____

_____

_____

_____

Going Further

Using the procedures presented in this investigation, test other species of bacteria—such as *B. subtilis*, *P. vulgaris*, and *S. lutea*—for their resistance or sensitivity to various disinfectants and antibiotics.

Investigating the Diversity of Protists

Introduction

Protists are members of the Kingdom Protista which includes unicellular and colonial organisms. Protists are very diverse in the ways that they live and acquire energy. They include autotrophs that produce food using photosynthesis and heterotrophs that feed on a variety of prey. The kingdom also includes slime molds that live as decomposers on rotting wood and rich soil. The diversity of feeding behaviors contributes to the complex protist food webs found in terrestrial and aquatic habitats. In this investigation you will learn about the feeding strategies of several protists.

Problem

What are the ways that fresh water protists can acquire energy for survival and how well are they equipped to compete with other aquatic species?

Pre-Lab Discussion

Read the entire investigation. Then, work with a partner to answer the following questions.

1. What is the technique that you will use to determine the population density of each species of protist you will use in your experiment on predator/prey relationships? Why is it necessary to do this?

   _____

   _____

   Why is it necessary to repeat the count several times?

   _____

2. What are some of the possible relationships that might exist between *Paramecia* and *Didinium*?

   _____

   _____

   _____

3. What would a positive attraction to light suggest about how a protist gets energy?

   _____

   _____

4. What would be a simple way to distinguish between an autotophic protist and a predatory protist?

   _____

5. What is the purpose of the card with the slit in the light sensitivity experiment?

Materials *(per group)*

living cultures of *Paramecium caudatum*, *Didinium*, *Blepharisma*, and *Euglena*
microscope slides
microscope
dropper pipette
coverslips
glass-marking pencil
metric ruler
methyl cellulose
index cards
scissors
test tubes
test-tube rack
plastic screening

Safety 🧤🔪🦠🔥

Put on a laboratory apron if one is available. Handle all glassware carefully. Always carry a microscope using two hands and place it securely on the table or work bench. Use caution with sharp instruments. Return or dispose of all materials according to the instructions of your teacher. Wash your hands thoroughly after working with microorganisms. Note all safety symbols in the Procedure and review the meaning of each symbol by referring to Safety Symbols on page 8.

Procedure

Part A: A Study of a Predator–Prey Relationship

 1. On two clean microscope slides, draw a 1-cm square using a glass-marking pencil. The square will make viewing of the organisms easier by preventing them from moving beyond its boundary.

2. Use a dropper pipette to place a drop of *Paramecium* culture on one of the slides. Add a drop of methyl cellulose to the slide to slow down the movement of the paramecia.

3. Using the low-power objective of the microscope, view the *Paramecium* culture. Count the number of paramecia that appear within the square. Record your observations in the Data Table. Wait 1 minute and then count the number of paramecia again. Wait another minute and count the number of paramecia a third time. Compute the average number of paramecia that appeared in the box at the three intervals of time.

Data Table

	Number of *Paramecium*	Number of *Didinium*
At start		
After 1 minute		
After 2 minutes		
Average		
After mixing species		
At start		
After 1 minute		
After 2 minutes		

4. Switch to the high-power objective. **CAUTION:** *When switching to the high-power objective, always look at the objective from the side of the microscope so that the objective does not hit or damage the slide.* Locate a single paramecium and observe its structure. Observe the method of movement the paramecium uses. Record your observations in the space below.

5. Repeat steps 2 through 4 using the *Didinium* culture. Record your results in the Data Table.

6. On a clean slide draw a 1-cm square using a glass-marking pencil. Add a drop of the *Paramecium* culture to the slide first and then a drop of the *Didinium* culture to the same square.

7. Observe the mixed cultures of *Paramecia* and *Didinium* at the start, after one minute, and after two minutes and record your results in the Data Table.

Part B: A Study of the Light Sensitivity of *Euglena* and *Blepharisma*

1. Trace the outline of a microscope slide onto an index card. Use scissors to cut out the outline. In the center of the cut-out piece, cut a slit about 2 cm long and 1 mm wide.

2. Place the card on the microscope stage with the slit over the opening of the microscope stage. Using the dropper pipette, place a drop of *Euglena* culture on a clean microscope slide. Add a drop of methyl cellulose to the slide to slow down the movement of the euglenas and apply a cover slip. Place the slide on top of the card on the microscope stage. Use the low power on the microscope to locate several euglenas.

3. Observe the euglenas that are visible through the slit. Wait about 30 seconds, then quickly remove the card. Record your observations on the following page.

4. Increase the magnification to 100X or 400X and locate a single euglena. **CAUTION:** *When switching to the high-power objective, always look at the objective from the side of the microscope so that the objective does not hit or damage the slide.* Locate a single euglena and observe its structure and the way that it moves.

5. Repeat steps 1–4 using the *Blepharisma* culture. Return your materials and wash your hands before leaving the laboratory.

Analysis and Conclusions

1. **Analyzing Data** In Part A, which protist was the predator and which was the prey? Explain your answer.

_____

_____

2. **Inferring** Based on your observations is a larger size a good indicator of a predatory species?

_____

_____

3. **Inferring** Which of the species that you examined is likely to be an autotroph? Explain your answer.

_____

_____

4. **Drawing Conclusions** Is *Euglena* a plantlike or animallike protist?

_____

_____

5. **Comparing and Contrasting** Three of the protists that you examined are called ciliates since they move by beating cilia. How would you categorize them according to their nutritional habits?

_____

_____

Going Further

Compare the sizes of *Didinium* and *Blepharisma*. If they have a predator-prey relationship how might it work? Mix a drop of the *Didinium* culture with a drop of the *Blepharisma* culture to determine whether they have a predator-prey relationship and if so, identify the predator.

Comparing the Characteristics of Molds

Introduction

Although often associated with food spoilage and the deterioration of wood, cloth, and other materials, molds and other fungi can be useful too. People take advantage of molds, for example, to produce a variety of cheeses. Penicillin, an important antibiotic, was originally made from *Penicillium* mold. Even citric acid, which is used in lemon-flavored candies and foods, may be made from *Aspergillus niger*, a black mold.

In this investigation, you will design and carry out an experiment to determine which conditions are favorable for the growth of molds.

Problem

What conditions are favorable for the growth of molds?

Pre-Lab Discussion

Read the entire investigation. Then, work with a partner to answer the following questions.

1. What is the purpose of the moist paper towel shown in Figure 1?

_____

_____

2. Have you ever found mold growing on food? Describe an environment where mold is likely to grow naturally on food.

_____

_____

_____

3. Write a hypothesis that you could test in this investigation.

_____

_____

_____

4. Make one prediction based on the hypothesis you wrote in 3 above.

_____

_____

_____

_____

_____

5. How might you test your prediction using the suggested materials? What results would support the hypothesis you wrote in 3?

_____

_____

_____

_____

Suggested Materials *(per group)*

paper towels
warm water
pieces of fruit, cheddar cheese, and bread
clear plastic bags
permanent marker
twist ties
hand lens
Request additional materials from your teacher
if you think you need them to carry out your experiment.

Safety 🜂 🜄 🜁 🜃 🜅 ⚠

Put on a laboratory apron if one is available. Put on safety goggles. Never taste anything used in this laboratory investigation. Follow your teacher's directions and all appropriate safety procedures when handling microorganisms. Wash your hands thoroughly each time you finish working with the materials. Note all safety symbols in Design Your Experiment and review the meaning of each symbol by referring to the Safety Symbols on page 8.

Design Your Experiment

1. Figure 1 shows one method for growing mold: Seal a food source and a moist paper towel in a clear plastic bag and place the bag in the desired environment for at least one week. **CAUTION:** *Do not open the bag, once it has been sealed. Treat all growth as a biohazard. At the end of the investigation, dispose of all bags as instructed by your teacher. Wash your hands thoroughly after preparing the bags and after each time you touch them.*

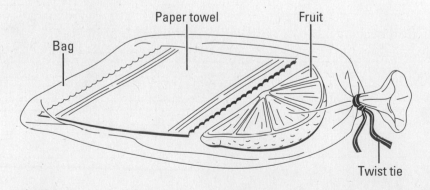

Figure 1

2. Choose at least one variable that you will test for its effect on mold growth. For example, you could examine the effects of temperature, moisture, light, or different food sources on mold growth.

_____

_____

_____

_____

3. Write a hypothesis about the variable(s) you will test for its effect on mold growth.

_____

_____

_____

_____

_____

4. Design an experiment to test the hypothesis you wrote in step 3. On the lines provided, describe the variables you will include in your experiment and the procedure you will follow. **Note:** *Do not carry out your experiment until your teacher has instructed you to do so.*

Manipulated variable(s)

_____

_____

_____

_____

Responding variable

_____

_____

_____

Controlled variables

_____

_____

_____

_____

_____

Procedure

_____

_____

_____

_____

_____

5. What safety precautions should you follow as you conduct the experiment you describe above?

_____

_____

_____

_____

6. Submit a written experimental plan to your teacher for approval. When your teacher has approved of your plan and given you permission to begin your experiment, carry out the experiment. **CAUTION:** *Put on a lab apron, safety goggles, and plastic gloves. Do not touch, taste, or smell the contents of the bags or open the bags for any reason, once they are sealed. Wash your hands thoroughly after preparing the bags and after each time the bags are touched. Treat the contents of the bags, once sealed, as a biohazard, and dispose of them according to your teacher's directions.*

7. Record your results in the Data Table provided or you may design your own data table. If you need more space, attach additional sheets of paper.

Data Table

Plastic bag	Type of food	Environment	Observations of growth (amount, color, texture)

Analysis and Conclusions

1. **Controlling Variables** What was the control in your experiment? Explain your answer.

   _____

   _____

   _____

   _____

2. **Evaluating and Revising** Look back at the hypothesis you tested in your experiment. Do your data support your hypothesis? Explain.

   _____

   _____

   _____

3. **Comparing and Contrasting** Based on the results of your experiment and those of your classmates, what conditions do you think are best for growing molds? Support your answer with data from the experiments.

   _____

   _____

   _____

   _____

   _____

4. **Drawing Conclusions** Based on the results of your experiment and those of your classmates, what can you do to inhibit the unwanted growth of molds on foods?

   _____

   _____

   _____

5. **Inferring** Athlete's foot is a condition caused by a fungus growing on human feet. Describe the conditions that might encourage the growth of this fungus and what can be done to prevent athlete's foot.

   _____

   _____

   _____

   _____

   _____

   _____

   _____

6. **Inferring** Molds sometimes grow on basement walls and floors, causing odors and damage. How can these problems be prevented?

_____

_____

_____

_____

Going Further

Seeds are often soaked in a slightly acidic solution in order to prevent mold from growing on them. Design an experiment to test whether slightly acidic solutions retard fungal growth.

Chapter 22   Plant Diversity

Comparing Green Algae and Mosses

Introduction

Algae are photosynthetic protists. Algae can be classified by color— green algae, brown algae, and red algae. Green algae can be unicellular or multicellular. Several species of unicellular algae, for example, the green species *Chlamydomonas*, can provide an idea of how multicellular plants may have evolved.

In contrast to the algae, mosses are land-dwelling plants. They are usually found in moist environments because they lack the water-conducting tubes found in higher plants. Instead, water passes from cell by cell through osmosis and surface tension around the stems. Since this method of transport only works well over short distances, these plants never grow very tall.

The first multicellular organisms evolved in water. Algae living today can give us some idea of what these first organisms were like. Over time, some organisms adapted to life in drier environments and evolved structures to acquire, transport, and conserve water. The mosses may represent one stage in this process, as they live in moist environments on the land. Algae and mosses are alike in that they lack specialized vascular tissues to transport water and the products of photosynthesis, but they differ in many ways. In this investigation you will compare a brown alga with moss.

Problem

How are brown algae and mosses similar and different?

Pre-Lab Discussion

Read the entire investigation. Then, work with a partner to answer the following questions.

1. What is the major difference between the habitats of brown algae and mosses?

_____

2. Which is closer to the ancestors of plants, algae or moss? Why do you think so?

_____

_____

_____

3. Examine the illustrations in Figures 1 and 3. How are the holdfast and the rhizoids similar?

_____

4. What is shown in Figures 2 and 4?

_____

5. Why is a water environment needed for sexual reproduction in both brown algae and mosses?

___

Materials *(per group)*

large shallow bowl
sea water
microscope
dissecting microscope
hand lens
dissecting tray
scissors
scalpel

microscope slide
coverslip
forceps
brown alga, *Fucus*
moss, *Polytrichum*
prepared slide of moss protonema
prepared slide of moss
    antheridia and archegonia

Safety 🔬🔪✂️

Put on a laboratory apron if one is available. Always handle the microscope with extreme care. You are responsible for its proper care and use. Use caution when handling microscope slides as they can break easily and cut you. Be careful when handling sharp instruments. Note all safety alert symbols next to the steps in the Procedure and review the meanings of each symbol by referring to Safety Symbols on page 8.

Procedure

Part A. Adaptive Structures and Reproduction of *Fucus* Algae

 1. Place the *Fucus* in a large shallow bowl. Cover the *Fucus* with sea water.

2. Carefully remove a piece of *Fucus* from the bowl and place it on the dissecting tray.

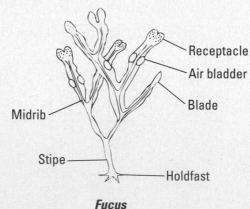

Fucus

Figure 1

3. Look for the main stem. At its base, notice a tough, fibrous pad of tissue called the holdfast.

4. Feel the stems in their midregions until you come across a small lump. This is the air bladder. Air bladders sometimes come in pairs on either side of the midrib.

5. Using the scissors, cut out a small section of the stem containing an air bladder. Place it back in the bowl and observe what happens.

6. Look at the leaflike structures on the seaweed. Find the flattened forked stem tips. Special cells called apical cells located at the tips divide by mitosis and produce the forked branching pattern.

7. Examine the stem tips for swollen areas called receptacles. Receptacles contain eggs and sperm.

8. Look for the most swollen receptacles because they are the most mature and are the best ones for examination. Orange-yellow receptacles contain gametes that are ready to be dispersed.

9. With a hand lens, notice the tiny bumps on the surface of a receptacle. For a closer look, use the dissecting microscope.

10. In order to examine the gametes, you will have to open the receptacles and look inside. Using a scalpel, carefully cut out a very thin cross section of the receptacle. See Figure 2.
    CAUTION: *Use extreme care when using a sharp instrument.*

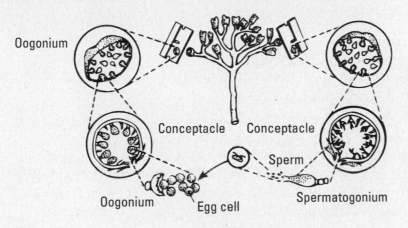

Life Cycle of *Fucus*

Figure 2

11. With the forceps, place the thin section of the receptacle on the microscope slide and prepare a wet mount.

12. Observe the section of the receptacle under the low power of the microscope. **Note:** *It may take a little practice to cut the section thin enough so that it can be viewed under the microscope.*

13. Inside the receptacle, look for several small, round chambers that come into contact with the receptacle. These chambers are called conceptacles. Notice whether a conceptacle has an opening to the outside wall. A female conceptacle has several round oogonial sacs, each of which contains 8 egg cells. A male conceptacle has spermatogonial sacs containing many orange dots. Each dot is a sperm cell. In *Fucus*, fertilization and development are external. In the space provided on page 175, sketch and label the conceptacle. Record the magnification.

Part B. Adaptive Structures and Reproduction of *Polytrichum* Moss

1. Examine a small clump of *Polytrichum* moss under the dissecting microscope. Use Figure 3 to identify the structures of a moss.

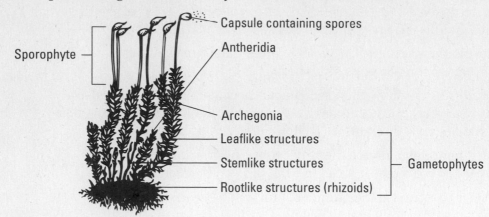

Polytrichum

Figure 3

2. Carefully separate a sporophyte from a gametophyte. A sporophyte consists of one stalk with a capsule on it. The green "leafy" part below the sporophyte is the female gametophyte. Notice that the capsule has a cap on it.

3. To examine the contents of the capsule, carefully remove the cap. Then place a drop of water on a microscope slide and squeeze the contents of the capsule into the water. Cover with a coverslip and locate the capsule's contents under low power. Then observe under high power. **CAUTION:** *When turning to the high-power objective lens, always look at the objective from the side of the microscope so that the objective lens does not hit or damage the slide.* In the space provided on page 175, sketch the spores. Record the magnification.

4. Examine a prepared slide of moss protonema. A protonema is a mass of tangled green filaments that grow from a spore.

5. Examine a prepared slide of moss antheridia and archegonia. These reproductive organs are found in the upper tips of the gametophytes.

6. Study Figure 4, which shows the life cycle of a moss. Compare the similarities and differences in the life cycles of *Fucus* and *Polytrichum*.

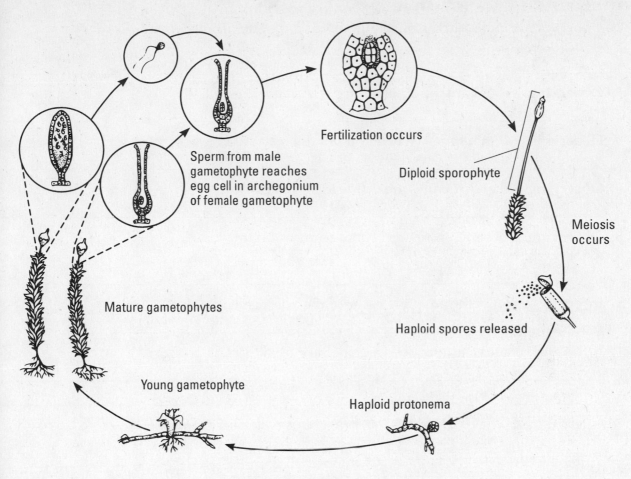

Fertilization occurs

Diploid sporophyte

Meiosis occurs

Haploid spores released

Sperm from male gametophyte reaches egg cell in archegonium of female gametophyte

Mature gametophytes

Young gametophyte

Haploid protonema

Life Cycle of *Polytrichum*

Figure 4

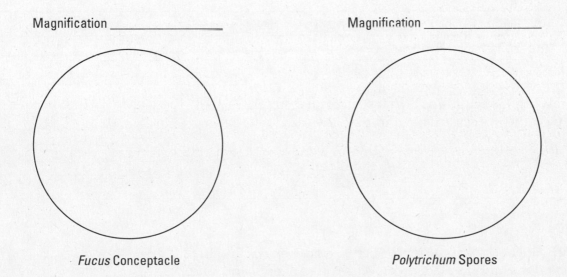

Magnification _____

Magnification _____

Fucus Conceptacle

Polytrichum Spores

Analysis and Conclusions

1. **Observing** What structure is found at the base of the main stem in a *Fucus* alga?

   _____

2. **Observing** Where are the air bladders found in *Fucus*?

   _____

3. **Observing** What happens when you put the *Fucus'* air bladder in water?

   _____

4. **Observing** What structures are inside the moss capsule?

   _____

5. **Observing** Does the protonema contain any structures? If so, what might they be?

   _____

6. **Inferring** What is the adaptive value of the holdfast on an alga?

   _____

7. **Inferring** What is the adaptive value of the air bladders on an alga?

   _____

   _____

8. **Inferring** Of what value is the flat, branching system of seaweed?

   _____

   _____

9. **Comparing and Contrasting** Compare the similarities and differences in the life cycles of *Fucus* and *Polytrichum*.

   _____

   _____

   _____

   _____

   _____

10. **Drawing Conclusions** What structural differences allow the moss to be more successful on land than the alga?

    _____

    _____

    _____

Going Further

Examine the external and reproductive structures of another land nonvascular plant, the liverwort *Marchantia*. Sketch and label what you see. Compare the structures of the liverwort with those you observed in the moss.

Observing Root and Stem Structures

Introduction

The first structures to appear on a germinating seed are the roots. The initial root to grow from a seed is the primary root, which is then followed by secondary roots that branch out from the primary root. In a taproot system, the primary root grows longer and thicker than the secondary roots. In a fibrous root system, the secondary roots continue to grow, and eventually all the roots are of equal or nearly equal size.

Roots anchor the plant in place, absorb water containing dissolved minerals from the environment, and act as storage areas for excess food. Adventitious roots grow from parts of the plant other than the roots. Aerial, or prop, roots are roots that are suspended in the air.

Plant structures that grow between the roots and leaves are called stems. Although stems usually grow above the ground in vertical positions, they can also grow under the ground in horizontal positions. All stems begin growing as soft, tubelike structures. If the stem remains soft, and usually green, for the entire life of the plant, it is a herbaceous stem. A woody stem becomes hard and often turns brown.

Stems conduct water and dissolved minerals from the roots to the leaves, and food from the leaves to the rest of the plant. Stems may also function as food storage areas, supporting structures, and places for the growth of new plants.

In this investigation, you will examine the structures of roots and stems. You will also observe the structural differences between some monocot and dicot roots and stems.

Problem

What are some structures of roots and stems?

Pre-Lab Discussion

Read the entire investigation. Then, work with a partner to answer the following questions.

1. Why is methylene blue stain used when the cross section of the carrot is observed?

_____

_____

_____

2. Why will you use a hand lens or a dissecting microscope rather than a compound light microscope to examine the cross section of carrot?

_____

_____

3. If you are given a stained cross section on a slide, how can you tell whether it is a section of root or of stem?

_____

_____

_____

4. Do root hairs appear to significantly increase the volume or the surface area of a root? What benefit does this increase provide for the plant?

_____

5. Which root type is more likely to be a food source—a fibrous root or a tap root? Explain your answer.

_____

Materials *(per group)*

2-week-old radish seedlings
hand lens or dissecting microscope
microscope
carrot
dissecting tray
scalpel or single-edged razor blade
forceps
microscope slide
gloves
dropper pipette
150-mL beaker
methylene blue stain
ethyl alcohol
prepared slides of cross section of:
    Helianthus root
    Zea root
    Helianthus stem
    Zea stem

Safety 🦶🥼🧤✋✂️♨️☣️🔥

Put on safety goggles. Put on a laboratory apron if one is available. Be careful to avoid breakage when working with glassware. Observe proper laboratory procedures when using electrical equipment. Always handle the microscope with extreme care. You are responsible for its proper care and use. Be careful when handling sharp instruments. Use caution when handling microscope slides as they can break easily and cut you. Always use special caution when working with laboratory chemicals, as they may irritate the skin or stain skin or clothing. Never touch or taste any chemical unless instructed to do so. Wash your hands thoroughly after carrying out this investigation. Note all safety alert symbols next to the steps in the Procedure and review the meanings of each symbol by referring to Safety Symbols on page 8.

Procedure

Part A. External and Internal Structures of a Root

1. Examine Figure 1 and identify each root as being taproot, fibrous, adventitious, or aerial. Write the correct root type in the blanks.

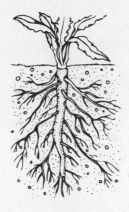
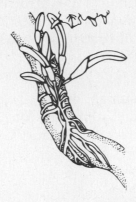
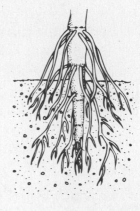

| Grass | Dandelion | Orchid | Corn |

Types of Roots

_____ _____ _____ _____

Figure 1

2. Examine the radish seedling. Note the basic structures of the seedling: leaves, stem, and roots.

3. With a hand lens or dissecting microscope, examine the delicate root hairs extending from the root.

4. Place the carrot in the dissecting tray. As shown in Figure 2, hold the carrot steady with one hand while you cut it in half lengthwise with the scalpel or single-edged razor blade. **CAUTION:** _Always cut in a direction away from yourself. Because the carrot is very hard, be careful not to let the scalpel or razor blade slip and cut you._

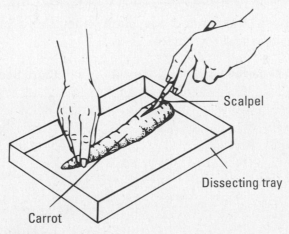

Scalpel

Dissecting tray

Carrot

Figure 2

5. Examine the two halves of the carrot. Each half is a longitudinal section. Notice the stele in the center. The stele contains the xylem and the phloem. Surrounding the stele is the food-storing cortex. In the labeled box, sketch a longitudinal section of the carrot. Label the stele and the cortex.

6. To make a cross section of the carrot, place one of the longitudinal sections cut side down on the dissecting tray. About 4 cm from the end of the carrot, cut straight down using the scalpel. Discard the small piece. **CAUTION:** *Be careful when handling a sharp instrument. Keep the scalpel well away from your fingers that are holding the carrot.*

7. Make another cut straight down, as close as possible to the one you just made. See Figure 3. With the forceps, carefully place the carrot cross section on a microscope slide. **CAUTION:** *Handle microscope slides carefully, as they can break easily and cut you.*

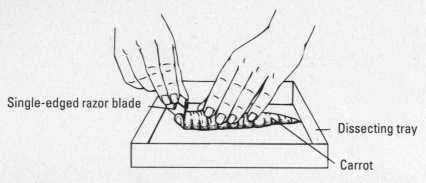

Single-edged razor blade

Dissecting tray

Carrot

Figure 3

8. Put on protective gloves. Place the slide over the mouth of the beaker. Then using a dropper pipette, cover the carrot cross section completely with methylene blue stain. Allow the stain to set for 1 minute. **CAUTION:** *Methylene blue stain is a permanent stain. Be careful not to get it on your hands or clothing.*

9. After 1 minute, slowly pour alcohol over the carrot cross section until no more stain washes away.

10. Observe the cross section of the carrot with a hand lens or under a dissecting microscope. In the labeled box, sketch the cross section of the carrot. Label the stele and the cortex.

Longitudinal Section of Carrot

Cross Section of Carrot

11. Place the prepared slide of the sunflower *(Helianthus)* root cross section under the low power of the microscope. The sunflower is a dicot. Locate the epidermal cells that form the outer edge of the root. Examine different areas on the glass slide. Notice some root hairs, which are extensions of single epidermal cells.

12. Find the cortex, which is located within the epidermis. The cells of the cortex are large and thin-walled.

13. Locate the star-shaped pattern formed by xylem cells at the center of the root. Switch to the high-power objective and focus on one xylem cell. Note its thick cell wall. **CAUTION:** *When switching to the high-power objective, always watch the nosepiece from the side to make certain that the objective does not hit or damage the slide.*

14. Observe the smaller and thinner-walled phloem cells between the arms of the star. This distinctive pattern of xylem and phloem is typical of dicot roots. In Figure 4, label the xylem, phloem, cortex, epidermis, and root hair.

15. Examine the corn *(Zea)* root cross section under the low power of the microscope. Corn is a monocot.

16. Notice that groups of xylem cells are scattered within the central area of the root. Move the microscope slide around until you find the phloem cells, which are also scattered in bunches through the central area of the root.

17. Notice that the cortex and epidermis are similar in both the sunflower root and the corn root. In Figure 5, label the xylem, phloem, cortex, epidermis, and root hair in the corn root.

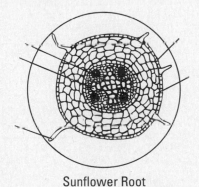

Sunflower Root

Figure 4

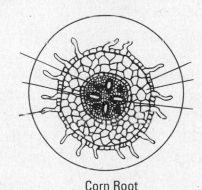

Corn Root

Figure 5

Part B. Internal Structures of Stems

1. Observe the prepared slide of a cross section of a sunflower *(Helianthus)* stem under low power of the microscope. The sunflower has a herbaceous, or nonwoody, stem. Notice that the vascular bundles are arranged in a ring within the stem. Switch to the high-power objective and focus on a single vascular bundle. Observe the thick-walled xylem cells. Notice the smaller, thinner-walled phloem cells within the bundle.

2. Switch back to the low-power objective and observe the arrangement of cells within the stem cross section. The pith is the large area within the ring of vascular bundles. Surrounding the ring is the cortex. The outermost layers are epidermis. In Figure 6, label the vascular bundle, xylem, phloem, pith, cortex, and epidermis.

3. Observe the prepared slide of a cross section of a corn (*Zea*) stem under the low-power objective of the microscope. Note the general arrangement of the cell and the position of the xylem and phloem.

4. Examine the epidermis, cortex, and pith in the corn stem cross section. In Figure 7, label the vascular bundle, xylem, phloem, epidermis, cortex, and pith.

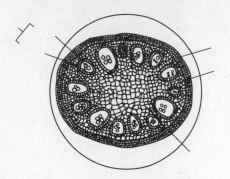

Figure 6   Sunflower Stem

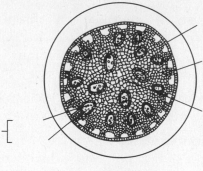

Figure 7   Corn Stem

Analysis and Conclusions

1. **Observing** In the cross sections of monocot and dicot roots that you observed, how were xylem and phloem arranged?

_____

_____

_____

2. **Compare and Contrast** Both roots and stems have a layer of epidermis that forms the outer layer of cells. How do the epidermal cells in roots differ in function from those in stems?

_____

_____

3. **Inferring** Which kind of root system would more likely benefit a desert plant—a taproot or a fibrous root system? Explain your answer.

_____

_____

Going Further

To observe how materials are transported up through a stem, cut the stem of a white carnation in half lengthwise. Measure out 50 mL of water into each of two beakers. Add 5 drops of red food coloring to one beaker and 5 drops of blue food coloring to the other beaker. Place the beakers side by side and carefully place one half of the carnation stem in each beaker. Allow the beakers to remain undisturbed for 24 hours. After 24 hours, observe the color of the carnation flower.

Name_____ Class_____ Date _____

Investigating Germination and Seedling Development

Introduction

When conditions are suitable, a seed undergoes germination, or the development of an embryo into a seedling. For germination to occur, water, warmth, and oxygen must be available in the proper amounts. The amounts vary from species to species.

Germination can occur only in viable seeds, or seeds in which the embryo is alive. Not all viable seeds will germinate, even when given the proper amounts of water, warmth, and oxygen. Many seeds must go through a period of dormancy, during which the embryo is alive but not growing. Dormancy is an adaptation that prevents germination of the seed until conditions are suitable.

In this investigation, you will observe some of the processes associated with seed germination and seedling development.

Problem

What changes occur in a seed during germination and seedling development?

Pre-Lab Discussion

Read the entire investigation. Then, work with a partner to answer the following questions.

1. What are the major environmental requirements for the germination of seeds.

_____

_____

2. Is a control needed for this study?

_____

_____

3. What is the advantage of using the *Brassica rapa* seeds for the study?

_____

_____

4. What parts of a new seedling are the hypocotyl, epicotyl, and primary root.

_____

_____

_____

_____

5. Why are no nutrients added to the water used to sprout the seeds?

_____

_____

Materials _(per pair)_

10 _Brassica rapa_ seeds
petri dish
forceps
hand lens
filter paper

fluorescent plant lamp (if available)
base of a 2-L soft-drink bottle
metric ruler

Safety 🔲 🔲

Handle all glassware carefully. Do not eat any materials such as the seeds provided by your teacher or the seedlings produced. Note all safety alert symbols next to the steps in the Procedure and review the meanings of each symbol by referring to Safety Symbols on page 8.

Procedure

1. As shown in Figure 1, use a metric ruler and pencil to draw a line across the filter paper about 3 cm from the top edge. Label the bottom edge of the filter paper with the seed type, date, and name of one member of your group. **Note:** _Be sure to use pencil to label the filter paper because ink will smear when water is added._

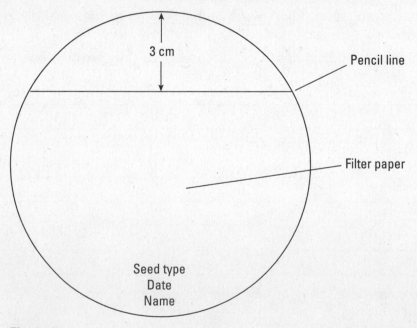

Figure 1

🔲 2. Place the filter paper in the top of a petri dish. Thoroughly wet the filter paper.

🔲 3. Use forceps to place 10 _Brassica rapa_ seeds on the line you drew on the filter paper. Space the seeds out evenly across the line as shown in Figure 2.

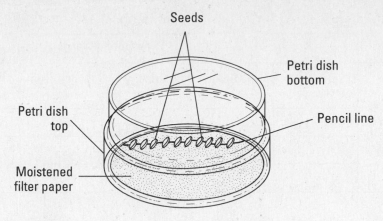

Figure 2

4. Cover the seeds by inserting the smaller bottom half of the petri dish into the top.

5. Carefully place the petri dish in the base of the 2-liter soft-drink bottle so that the seeds are at the top and the petri dish is tilted slightly. See Figure 3. Make sure that none of the seeds have fallen from their original positions. Slowly add water to the soft-drink bottle base from the side until the water reaches a depth of 2 cm.

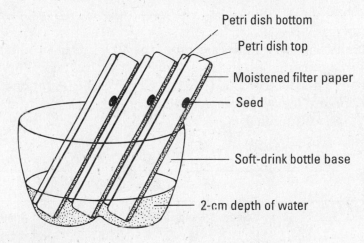

Figure 3

6. Place the soft-drink-bottle base under a fluorescent plant lamp. If a fluorescent lamp is not available, place the base near the best source of light in the room.

7. After 24 hours, observe the germination of the seeds. If necessary, use the hand lens to observe the germinating seeds. Note the number of seeds that have a split seed coat, an emerging radicle, hypocotyl, or epicotyl, or the appearance of a primary root and root hairs. Record the information in Data Table 1.

8. Measure the primary root length of each of the 10 seeds in millimeters and record this information in Data Table 2. If no primary root has emerged from a seed, record its length as 0 mm. Calculate the average root length for each of the 10 seeds and record this information in Data Table 2.

Data Table 1

| Time | Number of Seeds | | | | | |
	Split Seed Coat	Radicle	Primary Root	Root Hairs	Hypocotyl	Epicotyl
After 24 hours						
After 48 hours						
After 72 hours						

Data Table 2

| Time | Root Length (mm) | | | | | | | | | | |
	Seed 1	Seed 2	Seed 3	Seed 4	Seed 5	Seed 6	Seed 7	Seed 8	Seed 9	Seed 10	Average
After 24 hours											
After 48 hours											
After 72 hours											

9. Measure the hypocotyl length of each of the 10 seeds in millimeters and record this information in Data Table 3. If no hypocotyl has emerged from a seed, record its length as 0 mm. Calculate the average hypocotyl length for each of the 10 seeds and record this information in Data Table 3.

Data Table 3

| Time | Hypocotyl Length (mm) | | | | | | | | | | |
	Seed 1	Seed 2	Seed 3	Seed 4	Seed 5	Seed 6	Seed 7	Seed 8	Seed 9	Seed 10	Average
After 24 hours											
After 48 hours											
After 72 hours											

10. Repeat steps 8 and 9 after two more 24-hour periods. Record the information in Data Tables 1, 2, and 3.

11. On the graph on page 187, construct a line graph showing the average root length over the 72-hour observation period. On the same graph, construct a line graph showing the average hypocotyl length over the 72-hour observation period. Use pencils of different colors to construct the two line graphs. Label each line graph.

12. In the box labeled 72-hour-old *Brassica* seedling below, sketch one of your 72-hour-old seedlings. Label the hypocotyl, primary root, root hairs, cotyledons, and true leaves.

13. Calculate the growth rate of the root over the three days by dividing the average length by the period of time. For example 30 mm/3 days = 10 mm/day

14. Calculate the growth rate of the hypocotyl using the same method as above.

72-hour-old *Brassica* Seedling

Average length (mm) — *Time (hr)* graph with y-axis values 10, 20, 30, 40, 50, 60, 70, 80, 90, 100 and x-axis values 0, 24, 48, 72.

Analysis and Conclusions

1. **Observing** What is the first structure to emerge from inside the seed?

_____

_____

2. **Inferring** What is the function of this structure?

_____

_____

3. **Formulating Hypotheses** Why is it important for the dry seed to take in water before it begins to germinate?

_____

_____

_____

4. **Drawing Conclusions** How does a seedling benefit from having its radicle emerge before its leaves?

_____

_____

5. **Inferring** As the seedling grows, what part turns green and photosynthesizes?

_____

_____

Going Further

To observe the effect of light on seed germination and seedling development, prepare two petri dishes using the procedure described in this investigation. Completely wrap one of the dishes in aluminum foil and leave the other uncovered. Compare the rate of germination and the lengths of the primary roots and hypocotyls of the two sets of seeds. Construct data tables and compare the growth rates under the different conditions. You can also draw line graphs to show the growth rates. Write a simple summary of the results.

Investigating Germination Inhibitors

Introduction

Tomato seeds will usually germinate when exposed to the proper amounts of moisture and oxygen and a fairly warm temperature. Yet inside the tomato, where these conditions are also met, tomato seeds do not germinate. Why? Plants contain certain hormones that control their metabolism and growth processes.

In this investigation, you will first observe the effect of a germination inhibitor (a hormone) on seeds. You will then design and conduct an experiment to investigate the effect of a germination inhibitor from one variety of tomatoes on a second variety of tomatoes.

Problem

What are the effects of a germination inhibitor on seeds? What effect does a germination inhibitor from one variety of plant have on seeds of a different variety of the same species?

Pre-Lab Discussion

Read through the entire investigation. Then, work with a partner to answer the following questions.

1. Identify the manipulated and responding variables in Part A of this lab.

   _____

   _____

2. What is the purpose of petri dish 1 in the first experiment? Should a similar petri dish be set up when you design your experiment? Explain.

   _____

   _____

   _____

   _____

3. Explain how you can determine whether or not a seed has germinated.

   _____

   _____

4. Would it be possible to use a similar experiment to investigate the effect of a germination inhibitor from one variety of tomatoes on a second variety of tomatoes? How?

   _____

   _____

   _____

   _____

5. Discuss the possible outcomes of such an experiment (as discussed in Question 4) and explain the meaning of each.

_____

_____

_____

_____

_____

_____

Suggested Materials _(per group)_

tomatoes (2 different varieties)   beaker
filter paper   4 petri dishes
strainer   2 dropper pipettes
mortar and pestle (or bowl and spoon)   plastic wrap
funnel   glass-marking pencil

Safety 🔲🔳⚠

Put on a laboratory apron if one is available. Be careful to avoid breakage when working with glassware. Never touch or taste any chemical unless instructed to do so. Note all safety alert symbols next to the steps in Design Your Experiment and review the meanings of each symbol by referring to Safety Symbols on page 8.

Design Your Experiment

Part A. Observing the Effects of a Germination Inhibitor

🔲🔳 **1.** Put on your laboratory apron. With the glass-marking pencil, label two petri dishes 1 and 2.

2. Using a mortar and pestle, crush one whole tomato (Variety A). Strain the crushed tomato and use the funnel to collect the extract in the beaker. With a glass-marking pencil, label the beaker "Extract A" and set it aside for now.

3. From the tomato pulp, remove 20 seeds and wash them.

4. Line petri dishes 1 and 2 with filter paper. Place 10 seeds in each dish.

5. Use separate dropper pipettes to moisten petri dish 1 with water and petri dish 2 with the tomato extract. Cover the petri dishes with plastic wrap. Observe the seeds for several days, adding more water or tomato extract as needed to keep the filter paper moist.

6. Record the total number of seeds that germinate daily in each petri dish in the appropriate place in the Data Table.

Name_____ Class_____ Date _____

Data Table

Germination of Tomato Seeds								
Petri Dish	**Day 1**	**Day 2**	**Day 3**	**Day 4**	**Day 5**	**Day 6**	**Day 7**	**Day 8**
1 (Variety A with water)								
2 (Variety A with tomato extract)								

Part B. Your Own Experiment Plan an experiment to investigate the effect of a germination inhibitor from one variety of tomatoes on the germination of seeds of a second variety of tomatoes.

1. Write your hypothesis, identify the variables, and write out the procedure in the spaces below. Be sure to include a control in your experimental plan. Prepare a data table to record your data on a separate sheet of paper.

Hypothesis:

_____

_____

_____

_____

Manipulated variables:

_____

Responding variables:

_____

Controlled variables:

_____

Procedure:

_____

_____

_____

_____

_____

_____

_____

2. Submit your written experimental design to your teacher for approval. Once your design has been approved, carry out your experiment and record your data.

3. When you have finished your experiment, present the results of both experiments on the graph provided.

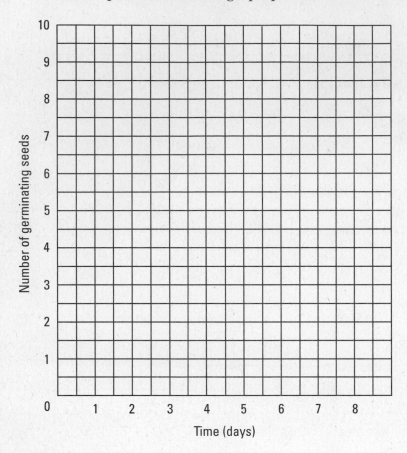

Analysis and Conclusions

1. **Analyzing Data** What were the results of Part A? How can you explain what occurred?

_____

_____

_____

_____

2. **Evaluating and Revising** Did the results of Part B support your hypothesis?

_____

_____

_____

_____

3. Drawing Conclusions What conclusions can be drawn from the data collected in both experiments?

_____

_____

_____

_____

_____

4. Formulating Hypotheses Based upon your observations, what function might germination inhibitors have?

_____

_____

_____

5. Inferring The seeds of a particular type of desert plant contain a water-soluble germination inhibitor. Only heavy rainfall causes the plant to germinate. Explain why this plant is well adapted to life in the desert.

_____

_____

_____

Going Further

What question(s) did the results of your experiment raise? Design an experiment that would address one of your questions or one that would logically follow this experiment.

Comparing Sponges and Hydras

Introduction

Sponges and cnidarians are simple invertebrates. Sponges make up the phylum Porifera, which means "pore-bearing." The phylum is named for the many pores that cover the body of a sponge. Cnidarians are members of the phylum Cnidaria. Hydras, jellyfishes, and sea corals are types of cnidarians.

Sponges have no true tissues or organs, no digestive tract, and no nervous system. Their bodies are loosely organized into two cell layers. Support comes from hard structures called spicules or from flexible material called spongin. Some sponges have both spicules and spongin.

Cnidarians have true tissues. Their bodies consist of two layers—an outer epidermis and an inner gastrodermis. Each cnidarian also has a body cavity where food is digested. Cnidarians have a simple nervous system that allows them to respond to stimuli.

In this investigation, you will examine the characteristics of sponges and cnidarians.

Problem

What are some characteristics of a sponge and a hydra?

Pre-Lab Discussion

Read the entire investigation. Then, work with a partner to answer the following questions.

1. Sponges are filter feeders that consume microscopic particles of food. Since sponges do not have mouths, what body structures would you expect to find that enable them to feed?

_____

_____

2. Why were sponges once thought to be plants? How will you be able to use the results of this investigation to prove to someone that sponges are *not* plants?

_____

_____

3. In Part A, why will you add the chlorine bleach solution to a piece of sponge?

_____

_____

4. How are the habitats of sponges and hydras similar? Would this lead you to expect similar body structures? Explain your answer.

_____

_____

_____

5. Like most cnidarians, hydras use stinging structures to capture small animals. Where would you expect to find these stinging structures?

_____

_____

Materials _(per group)_

preserved whole specimen of _Grantia_
prepared slide of _Grantia_, longitudinal section
hand lens
microscope
scalpel or single-edged razor blade
glass slide
coverslip
chlorine bleach solution
toothpick
2 dropper pipettes
prepared slide of hydra, whole mount
prepared slide of hydra, longitudinal section

Safety 🔲🧤🥽✂️🧪

Put on a laboratory apron if one is available. Put on safety goggles. Handle all glassware carefully. Always use special caution when working with laboratory chemicals, as they may irritate the skin or cause staining of the skin or clothing. Never touch or taste any chemical unless instructed to do so. Always handle the microscope with extreme care. You are responsible for its proper care and use. Use caution when handling microscope slides as they can break easily and cut you. Be careful when handling sharp instruments. Always use special caution when working with laboratory chemicals. Never touch or taste any chemical unless instructed to do so. Note all safety symbols next to the steps in the Procedure and review the meanings of each symbol by referring to Safety Symbols on page 8.

Procedure

Part A. Examining the Anatomy of a Sponge

1. With a hand lens, examine the external structure of the simple marine sponge *Grantia*. Find the osculum, which is a large opening at the top through which water flows out of the sponge. Locate several ostia (singular, ostium), or pore cells. Water flows into the sponge through the ostia. Note the long, straight spicules that encircle the osculum and project through the outer surface of the sponge. In the box labeled *Grantia*, sketch what you see. Label the osculum, ostia, and spicules.

2. Under the low-power objective of a microscope, examine a prepared slide of a longitudinal section of *Grantia*. Note the two cell layers. The outer cell layer is called the ectoderm and the inner cell layer is called the endoderm. Look for the flagellated cells called collar cells in the endoderm. Collar cells collect food particles from the water that passes through the sponge's body cavity, or spongocoel. Between the ectoderm and the endoderm is mesenchyme, or a jellylike material containing some cells. Observe the spicules, hard structures made of calcium carbonate. In the circle labeled *Grantia*, Longitudinal Section, sketch the sponge you have observed under low power. Label the ectoderm, mesenchyme, collar cell, flagellum, spicules, and spongocoel. Record the magnification of the microscope.

Grantia

3. Using a scalpel or a single-edged razor blade, cut a small piece from the *Grantia* specimen. **CAUTION:** *Be very careful when handling sharp instruments. Always cut in a direction away from your hands and body.*

4. Put on safety goggles. Place the piece of *Grantia* on a microscope slide. With a dropper pipette, add two drops of chlorine bleach solution to the piece of sponge. **CAUTION:** *Be very careful when using chlorine bleach. It may burn your skin or clothing.* Using a toothpick, gently stir the sponge and chlorine bleach solution.

5. Using another dropper pipette, add a drop of water to the slide. Then cover with a coverslip. Observe the *Grantia* spicules under the low-power objective of the microscope. In the circle labeled *Grantia* Spicules, sketch several spicules. Record the magnification of the microscope.

Magnification _____

Magnification _____

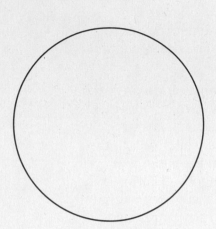

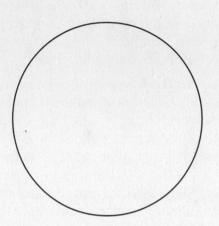

Grantia, Longitudinal Section

Grantia Spicules

Part B. Examining the Anatomy of a Hydra

1. Under low power of the microscope, examine a prepared, whole mount slide of a hydra. Locate the basal disk at the posterior end of the body. The basal disk is the part with which the hydra attaches itself to surfaces. At the anterior end is the mouth. Look for several long tentacles. In the circle labeled Hydra, Whole Mount, sketch the hydra under low power. Label the mouth, tentacle, body, and basal disk.

Magnification _____

Magnification _____

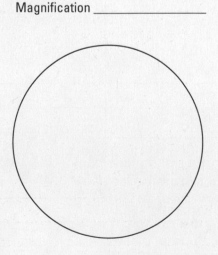

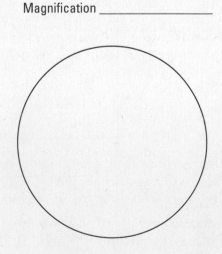

Hydra, Whole Mount

Hydra, Longitudinal Section

2. Under low power of the microscope, examine a prepared slide of a longitudinal section of a hydra. Locate the three layers: the outer epidermis, the inner gastrodermis, and the mesoglea, or thin layer of jellylike material between the epidermis and gastrodermis. Note the body cavity called the gastrovascular cavity.

3. Locate one of the hydra's tentacles. Notice the small bumps on the tentacle. They contain stinging structures called nematocysts.

4. Most species of hydra have separate male and female animals. However, some species contain both male and female reproductive structures. Look for the testes, or cone-shaped structures found on the upper half of the body, and the ovary, found on the lower half of the body. Examine the hydra to see if it has testes or an ovary (or both). In the circle labeled Hydra, Longitudinal Section, sketch the hydra under low power. Label the mouth, tentacle, nematocyst, testis (if present), ovary (if present), bud (if present), epidermis, mesoglea, gastrodermis, and gastrovascular cavity.

Analysis and Conclusions

1. **Inferring** What is the function of the spicules of a sponge?

_____

_____

2. **Drawing Conclusions** What body structures make the sponge well adapted for living in water?

_____

_____

3. **Inferring** What is the function of the gastrovascular cavity of a hydra?

_____

_____

4. **Comparing and Contrasting** Compare the sponge and the hydra in terms of body symmetry and tissue structure.

_____

_____

_____

5. **Comparing and Contrasting** How do sponges differ from flagellate protists?

_____

_____

_____

6. **Inferring** Why do you think a *Grantia* sponge should not be used to wash cars or porcelain sinks?

_____

_____

_____

7. **Classifying** "Cnid" is the Greek word for nettle, or stinging hair. Is the phylum name Cnidaria appropriate to the group of organisms such as hydra and jellyfishes? Explain your answer.

_____

_____

_____

_____

Going Further

To examine the feeding habits of the hydra, place several drops of hydra culture that has remained unfed for 24 hours in a watch glass. Add a drop of *Daphnia* culture to the watch glass. Place the watch glass under a dissecting microscope for observation. Describe what you see.

Observing the Structure of a Squid

Introduction

You are probably familiar with clams, snails, slugs, squids, and octupuses, and you probably have noticed how very different they are. Nevertheless, all these are classified in the phylum Mollusca. You will be examining one type of mollusk—a squid. Squids have some characteristics in common with other mollusks, but they also have special features that make them unique. Squids are classified in the class Cephalopoda. In this investigation, you will be examining a squid to find out why squids are classified as mollusks. You will also determine what special adaptations make them different from other mollusks.

Problem

What evidence is there that squids are mollusks? What adaptations make them different from other mollusks?

Pre-Lab Discussion

Read through the entire investigation. Then, work with a partner to answer the following questions.

1. To what kingdom do mollusks belong?

   _____

2. Describe the characteristics that organisms classified in phylum Mollusca share.

   _____

   _____

3. Name some organisms that belong to the phylum Mollusca.

   _____

   _____

4. Explain the characteristics that squids possess that lead to their classification as Cephalopods.

   _____

   _____

   _____

   _____

5. What other organisms belong to the Cephalopod class and why?

   _____

   _____

   _____

   _____

Materials *(per pair)*

squid
dissecting tray
dissecting pins
compound microscope
microscope slide
coverslip
dropper pipette
metric ruler
dissecting probe
scissors
hand lens
forceps
unlined white paper

Safety 🔥👓🧤✋✂️🔪

Put on a laboratory apron if one is available. Put on safety goggles and plastic gloves. Always handle the microscope with extreme care. You are responsible for its proper care and use. Use caution when handling microscope slides as they can break easily and cut you. Be careful when handling sharp instruments. Dispose of the squid specimen as instructed by your teacher. Wash your hands thoroughly when you are finished working with the materials. Note all safety symbols in the Procedure and review the meanings of each symbol by referring to Safety Symbols on page 8.

Procedure

1. Obtain a squid specimen in a dissecting tray. Count the number of arms and tentacles. Using a hand lens, examine the suckers on the arms. In the space provided below, sketch one sucker.

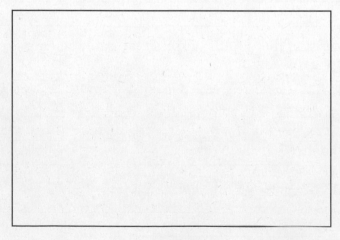

Sucker

2. Study the two longer, grasping tentacles and the sleek body with its pairs of fins and eyes. Place your squid on its dorsal surface. Locate the mantle, a loose edge of tissue near the eyes, and identify the siphon, noting it can be moved in any direction. In the space provided, make a careful sketch of the specimen, labeling the mantle, lateral fin, siphon, eye, tentacles, arms, and suckers.

3. Using the metric ruler, measure the length and width of your specimen in centimeters and record these measurements with your sketch.

Length of Squid _____

External Anatomy of a Squid

4. With forceps, lift the free end of the mantle just above the siphon, and using scissors, cut through the mantle in a straight line to the pointed end of the body. **CAUTION:** *Be careful when handling sharp instruments. Always cut in a direction away from your hands and body.* Spread the mantle, and with dissecting pins, secure it to the tray. Trace the siphon backward, using a dissecting probe to move aside the muscles that are attached to and control the siphon. Wastes, ink, and gametes are carried out of the squid by a current of water that leaves through the muscular siphon.

5. Examine the digestive system. Using scissors, start cutting at the neck and continue cutting through the head to a point midway between but just past the eyes, where you will reach a rough, muscular organ that surrounds the jaws. Push a probe between the jaws to locate the mouth.

6. Find the esophagus, a narrow tube below the jaws. Trace it to the stomach. Food moves through the esophagus, passing briefly through a junction with the liver before entering the stomach. The cecum is an elongated pouch off the stomach where absorption occurs. See if you can identify these structures. Follow the narrow tube, or intestine, from the cecum to the anus. Identify the dark ink sac near the anus. **Note:** *Do not puncture the ink sac at this time.*

7. Examine the respiratory system. Locate the gills, which look like curved feathers, one on each side of the body. Using forceps, transfer a tiny piece of gill to a microscope slide. Add a drop of water and a coverslip, and observe the tissue under the low-power and then the high-power objective of your microscope. In the space provided below, sketch what you see.

Squid Gill

8. Find the systemic heart of the circulatory system, which is located where the gill attaches to the body.

9. Locate the excretory system, which consists of two small triangular bodies at the base of the gills. In the space provided below, make a careful sketch of the internal organs, labeling the parts of the digestive, respiratory, circulatory, and excretory systems that you have been asked to identify above.

Internal Organs of a Squid

10. To locate the internal skeleton, cut through the mantle between the eyes and look for a small, plastic-like structure called a pen.

11. Determine the sex of your specimen by observing the fifth pair of arms. In a female, there is a small pouch or fold between these arms, while in the male, the fifth pair is modified to transfer sperm to the female. Inside the pointed section of the body, locate the sticky gonad, posterior to the kidneys. Observe the specimen of another lab group so you have a chance to examine squids of both sexes. Identify the sex of your specimen and record your observations.

12. Squids have an excellent nervous system, which includes one pair of eyes. Using a hand lens, study one eye, noting the covering, or cornea. Record your observations.

13. Before completing the dissection, carefully puncture the ink sac with a dissecting probe and use the ink and the probe to write your name on an unlined piece of paper. Record your observations.

14. Discard your specimen as instructed by your teacher. Wash your hands thoroughly when you are finished with the materials.

Analysis and Conclusions

1. **Analyzing Data** Based upon your examination of the squid, what features explain its classification as a mollusk?

_____

_____

_____

_____

_____

2. **Analyzing Data** What features did you observe that are unusual for a mollusk? What function does each serve?

_____

_____

_____

_____

3. **Drawing Conclusions** Often in biological systems, structure is said to be related to function. Describe the structure of the gills and explain how they are specialized for their function.

_____

_____

_____

_____

4. **Drawing Conclusions** Based upon your observations, what structures of a squid are specialized for movement?

_____

_____

_____

_____

5. **Inferring** How do the external and internal anatomy of a squid reflect its life as a predator?

_____

_____

_____

_____

_____

Going Further

Study the composition of the squid's ink. Transfer some of the ink from the ink sac to a small test tube. Test the ink for the presence of proteins, fats, starches, and sugars to determine its composition. Report on your findings.

Investigating Insect Metamorphosis

Introduction

As insects develop from eggs to adults, they pass through complete or incomplete metamorphosis. Butterflies and beetles are examples of insects that have an active larval stage that does not resemble the adult insect. See Figure 1. The mealworm beetle undergoes complete metamorphosis. The larva, mealworms and adult beetles eat different things. And like other insects, they do not maintain a constant internal body temperature. Instead, their body temperature usually depends on the temperature of their surroundings. As the seasons change, the foods available and the surrounding temperatures also change. It may be that the mealworm life cycle is controlled by the temperature and the food that is available during the year. In this investigation, you will design an experiment to determine how temperature affects the development of mealworms.

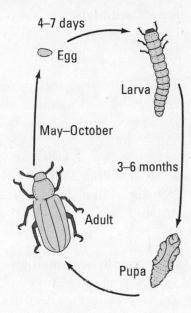

Mealworm Life Cycle

Figure 1

Pre-Lab Discussion

Read the entire investigation. Then, work with a partner to answer the following questions.

1. What characteristic of mealworms makes it likely that temperature affects their rate of development?

_____

_____

2. What are some distinguishing anatomical characteristics of insects?

_____

_____

_____

3. At what time of year do the beetles usually appear?

_____

4. Which of the stages is likely to end because of a drop in temperature?

_____

5. How do the adult beetles differ from the larvae?

_____

Suggested Materials *(per group)*

hand lens or dissecting microscope
mealworms in egg, larva, pupa, and adult stages
oatmeal
pieces of fresh apple or potato
plastic containers with loose fitting lids for ventilation
small plastic cups for moving and observing animals

Safety 🧤🥽🧫🔬

In this investigation, you will be observing living organisms. Treat all containers of living organisms as if they are hazardous. Follow your teacher's directions and all appropriate safety procedures when handling live animals. Always handle the microscope with extreme care. You are responsible for its proper care and use. Wash your hands at the end of the lab if you handle the insects. Note all safety alert symbols next to the steps in Design Your Experiment and review the meanings of each symbol by referring to Safety Symbols on page 8.

Design Your Experiment

1. Working in teams, use the hand lens or dissecting microscope to examine the various stages of the mealworm life cycle. Use the space below and on page 209 to make drawings and to list as many observations as you can make (shape, senses, movement, and so on) about the four stages of the mealworm life cycle. Consider ways to study the physical and behavioral capacities of the larvae and adults. Use additional sheets of paper if necessary.

Drawings of Mealworms in Different Stages

Name_____ Class_____ Date_____

Mealworm Characteristics

_____

_____

_____

_____

_____

_____

2. Use your textbook or other resources as references to label the parts of the insects in your drawings.

3. Design an experiment to see if temperature affects the rate of metamorphosis from the mealworm stage to the beetle stage. Describe your experimental design in the spaces below and create any data tables that you may need. Your class may wish to pool their data and construct a graph of the results. Obtain your teacher's permission before performing your experiment.

Hypothesis:

_____

_____

_____

_____

_____

Manipulated Variables:

_____

Responding Variables:

_____

Controlled Variables:

_____

Procedure:

_____

_____

_____

_____

_____

_____

_____

Analysis and Conclusions

1. **Observing** What are some anatomical characteristics of the larvae that show that they are arthropods and not annelid worms?

_____

_____

2. **Analyzing Data** Evaluate the class data on the effects of temperature on metamorphosis. At what temperature did the fastest insect metamorphosis occur? At which temperature did the slowest metamorphosis occur?

_____

_____

_____

3. **Inferring** Propose an explanation for the effect of temperature on the rate of insect metamorphosis.

_____

_____

_____

_____

4. **Interpreting Graphics** Does the seasonal life cycle of the mealworm beetle seem consistent with the effects of temperature on metamorphosis that you observed?

_____

_____

_____

5. **Predicting** Would a very cold winter as opposed to a mild one make any difference in the number of insects observed the next summer? Explain your answer.

_____

_____

_____

_____

Going Further

Collect some larvae from a rotten or decaying log and establish them in a laboratory culture. Observe their metamorphosis cycle. Describe your results.

Name_____ Class_____ Date _____

Comparing Invertebrate Body Plans

Introduction

Invertebrates, like all other organisms, are divided into groups based on certain distinguishing characteristics. Two characteristics that are examined when grouping invertebrates are cell layers and body cavities.

The number of cell layers making up the body varies among invertebrates. Cnidarians—jellyfishes and sea anemones, for example—possess only two cell layers in their body wall: an inner gastroderm and an outer epidermis. Other invertebrates—worms, mollusks, arthropods, and echinoderms, to name a few—have three basic cell layers: an inner endoderm, a middle mesoderm, and an outer ectoderm.

The animals that possess three basic cell layers can be divided into groups based on the structure of their body cavity. The body cavity, if present, is a fluid-filled hollow in the body wall that is located between the endoderm and the ectoderm. Animals that lack a body cavity are called acoelomates. Animals that have a body cavity that is only partially lined with mesoderm are called pseudocoelomates. And animals that have a body cavity that is completely lined with mesoderm are called coelomates.

In this investigation, you will compare the body plans and structures of invertebrates from four different phyla.

Problem

What are the differences in body plans and structures of the cnidarians, flatworms, roundworms, and annelids?

Pre-Lab Discussion

Read the entire investigation. Then, work with a partner to answer the following questions.

1. Which organisms will you observe in this investigation? Will you be observing live organisms?

   _____

   _____

   _____

2. How will you be able to tell whether each organism has a coelom or a pseudocoelom?

   _____

   _____

   _____

   _____

3. Which organisms do you expect to have a coelom or a pseudocoelom?

_____

_____

_____

4. List two advantages a coelom might provide an organism.

_____

_____

_____

5. Suppose a new phylum of invertebrates is discovered. These newly discovered invertebrates have a gastrovascular cavity and a very thin layer of mesodermal cells but show no organ development. Where would you place this new phylum on a phylogetic tree with respect to the four phyla represented in this investigation?

_____

_____

_____

Materials *(per group)*

microscope
prepared slides of cross sections of:
   cnidarian *(Hydra)*
   flatworm *(Dugesia)*
   roundworm *(Ascaris lumbricoides)*
   earthworm *(Lumbricus terrestris)*

Safety 🔦🔬

Be careful to avoid breakage when working with glassware. Always handle the microscope with extreme care. You are responsible for its proper care and use. Observe proper laboratory procedures when using electrical equipment. Use caution when handling glass slides as they can break easily and cut you. Note all safety symbols next to the steps in the Procedure and review the meanings of each symbol by referring to Safety Symbols on page 8.

Procedure

Part A. Examining the Body Plan and Structures of the Cnidarian

   1. Examine Figure 1 on page 213, which shows the basic body plans of the four invertebrates you will be examining.

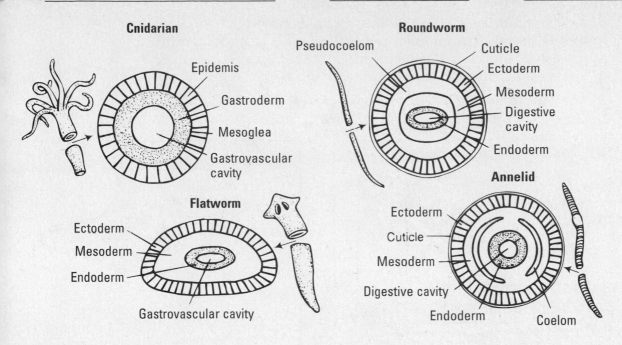

Figure 1

2. Examine a prepared slide of a cross section of a cnidarian under the low-power objective of a microscope. Look at the body layers. Switch to high-power to see the specific structures in greater detail. **Note:** *When switching to the high-power objective, always look at the objective from the side of the microscope so that the objective does not hit or damage the slide.* **CAUTION:** *Microscope slides have sharp edges and can break. Always handle the microscope with extreme care and do not use it around water or with wet hands. Never use direct sunlight as the light source for the microscope.*

3. Locate the epidermis, or outer layer of cells. Try to find some barbed cells called cnidocytes, each of which contains a stinging structure called a nematocyst.

4. Locate the gastroderm, or inner cell layer. Notice how some of the cells in the gastroderm have flagella. These flagellated cells help to circulate food and other materials within the gastrovascular cavity.

5. Locate the gastrovascular cavity in the center of the cross section of the cnidarian. Food digestion occurs within the gastrovascular cavity.

6. Locate the mesoglea, which is a noncellular, jellylike material between the epidermis and the gastroderm.

7. Label the following structures on the cross section of the cnidarian *(Hydra)* in Figure 2 on page 214: epidermis, mesoglea, gastroderm, cnidocyte, nematocyst, and gastrovascular cavity.

Part B. Observing the Body Plan and Structures of the Flatworm

1. Examine a prepared slide of a cross section of a flatworm under low power. Locate the ectoderm, endoderm, and gastrovascular cavity.

2. Find the middle cell layer, or mesoderm, between the ectoderm and the endoderm. The mesoderm makes up most of the flatworm and consists of muscles, glands, organs, loose cells, and many other kinds of structures. Notice the absence of a body cavity.

3. Label the following structures on the cross section of the flatworm in Figure 3: ectoderm, mesoderm, endoderm, and gastrovascular cavity.

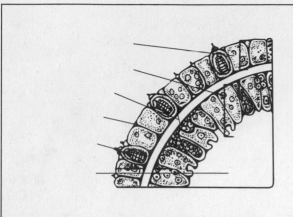

Cross Section of Cnidarian (Hydra)

Figure 2

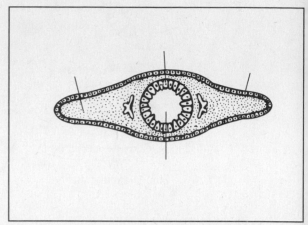

Cross Section of Flatworm (Dugesia)

Figure 3

Part C. Examining the Body Plan and Structures of the Roundworm

1. Examine a prepared slide of a cross section of a roundworm under low power. Locate the thick outer covering called the cuticle. This tough coating keeps a parasitic roundworm from being digested by its host. Just inside of the cuticle is the ectoderm, a thin layer of cells. Locate the mesoderm, the fiberlike layer just inside the epidermis.

2. Toward the center of the roundworm, look for the endoderm. The space inside the endoderm is the inside of the roundworm's digestive tract. The space between the endoderm and the mesoderm is called a pseudocoelom.

3. Label the following structures on the cross section of the roundworm in Figure 4: cuticle, ectoderm, mesoderm, endoderm, and pseudocoelom.

Part D. Examining the Body Plan and Structures of the Earthworm

1. Examine a prepared slide of a cross section of an earthworm. Find the thin protective outer layer called the cuticle. Just below the cuticle, look for the layer of cells of the ectoderm.

2. Inside the ectoderm are two muscle layers. The outer layer contains the circular muscles, which run circularly around the earthworm. The thick inner layer contains the longitudinal muscles, which run the length of the worm. These two layers of muscle make up the mesoderm.

3. Examine the center of the slide. You will see a round or horseshoe-shaped space that is the inside of the digestive tract. The layer of cells that surrounds the space is the endoderm. Surrounding the endoderm is another set of circular and longitudinal muscles.

4. Notice a relatively open space between the muscles surrounding the digestive tract and the muscles just inside the epidermis. This body cavity is called a coelom.

5. Locate a long, fiberlike structure inside the coelom. This structure, called a nephridium, is involved in excretion. There should be one nephridium on each side of the earthworm's body.

6. On the outer surface of the earthworm, find some bristly structures called setae. The earthworm uses the setae to help move its body through the soil.

7. Label the following structures on the cross section of the earthworm in Figure 5: cuticle, ectoderm, circular and longitudinal muscles (both sets), endoderm, coelom, nephridium, and setae.

Cross Section of Roundworm (Ascaris)
Figure 4

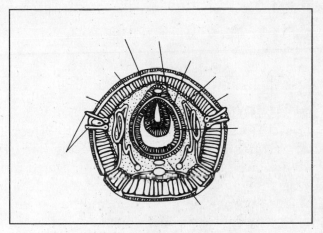

Cross Section of Earthworm (Lumbricus)
Figure 5

Analysis and Conclusions

1. **Inferring** What structures in the cnidarian correspond to the digestive cavity, ectoderm, and endoderm in the earthworm?

_____

_____

_____

2. **Comparing and Contrasting** How is the body plan of the cnidarian different from the body plan of the flatworm?

_____

_____

_____

3. **Comparing and Contrasting** How is the body plan of the flatworm similar to the body plan of the roundworm? How is the body plan of the flatworm different from the body plan of the roundworm?

_____

_____

_____

4. **Classifying** Suppose a newly discovered organism is found to have three body layers. Scientists think that it is a worm but disagree as to the group in which it should be placed. How could they assign it to the proper group based on body structure?

_____

_____

_____

5. **Comparing and Contrasting** How is the body plan of the earthworm different from the body plans of the other three organisms you examined?

_____

_____

_____

Going Further

Construct or draw a new form of invertebrate having characteristics of one existing phylum or of intermediate characteristics between two related phyla. From your completed model or drawing, your classmates should be able to identify the animal's symmetry, locomotion, nervous system, method of circulation, excretory system, and type of digestive system and, based upon its gas-exchange structure, whether your new "species" is terrestrial or aquatic.

Investigating Frog Anatomy

Introduction

Frogs are typical amphibians, adapted to live in water and on land. The organization of an adult frog's internal organs is similar to the internal organization of other vertebrates that live on land. Its small size makes it easy to study. In this investigation you will dissect an adult frog and observe structures that make the frog adapted to its environment.

Problem

What are some features of a frog's anatomy that help it adapt to its environment?

Pre-Lab Discussion

Read the entire investigation. Then, work with a partner to answer the following questions.

1. What will you examine in Part A of this investigation?

   _____

2. Why is it important to make shallow cuts when cutting the skin around the frog's hindlimb?

   _____

   _____

3. After you expose the internal organs in Part B, what two structures might you have to remove in order to examine the organs?

   _____

   _____

4. Which organs of the digestive system will you identify in Part C?

   _____

   _____

5. Without the presence of eggs, how will you know whether your frog is male or female?

   _____

Materials (per pair)

preserved frog   forceps
paper towels   plastic food bag
dissecting tray   dissecting pins
dissecting scissors   waterproof marker
dissecting probes

Safety

Put on safety goggles. Put on a laboratory apron and disposable plastic gloves, if they are available. Treat the preserved animal, preservation solution, and all equipment that touches the organism as potential hazards. Do not touch your eyes or your mouth with your hands. Be careful when handling sharp instruments. Return or dispose of all materials according to the instructions of your teacher. Wash your hands thoroughly after carrying out this investigation. Note all safety symbols next to the steps in the Procedure and review the meanings of each symbol by referring to Safety Symbols on page 8.

Procedure

Part A. The Head and Limbs

1. Work in pairs throughout this investigation. Wear your safety goggles, laboratory apron, and disposable gloves. Obtain a preserved frog from your teacher. Rinse the frog with water to wash off as much preservative as possible and then blot it dry with a paper towel. Place the frog in the dissecting tray and briefly examine it. **CAUTION:** *When working with preserved organisms, do not touch your eyes or mouth with your hands.*

2. Examine the frog's head. Notice the size and position of the eyes. The round, flattened areas of skin behind the eyes are the eardrums. The two holes near the mouth are the nostrils, called the external nares.

3. To examine the interior of the mouth, pry open the mouth and use the scissors to cut the edges of the mouth at each hinge joint, as shown in Figure 1. **CAUTION**: *Handle sharp tools carefully.* Insert the dissecting probe into both external nares. The openings inside the mouth through which the probe emerges are the internal nares. Along the rim of the mouth you will find a row of small maxillary teeth. Farther back, attached to the roof of the mouth, are two sharp vomerine teeth.

4. Find the wide opening in the center of the mouth. This is the top of the esophagus—the tube that leads to the frog's stomach. Below the esophagus is a vertical slit called the glottis—the tube that leads to the lungs.

5. Use a dissecting probe to move the frog's tongue. Note where the tongue is attached to the jaw.

6. On page 222, label each part of the frog's mouth on the lines provided.

7. Examine the frog's forelimbs and hindlimbs. Observe the webbed toes. Compare the sizes of the muscles on the front and back limbs.

8. With the point of your scissors, carefully make an incision through the skin where one of the hindlimbs joins the body. If necessary, use the forceps to pull up the skin. Cut the skin around the hindlimb as shown in Figure 2. **Note:** *The frog's skin is very thin. When cutting the skin, make shallow cuts to avoid damaging the muscles under the skin.* With the forceps, peel the skin off the hindlimb to expose the muscles underneath. Gently remove the thin, connective tissue covering the muscles. The muscles are connected to the bones with tough white cords called tendons. When a muscle contracts, the tendon moves and pulls the bone.

Carefully cut the edges of the mouth at each hinge joint.

Figure 1

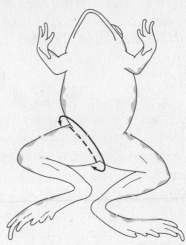

Carefully cut the skin around one hindlimb. Make shallow cuts to avoid damaging muscles.

Figure 2

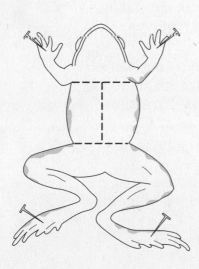

Gently lift the loose skin where the hindlimbs meet. Carefully make an incision through the raised skin.

Figure 3

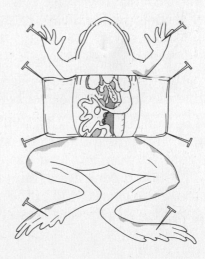

Lift the skin flaps and pin them to the wax.

Figure 4

9. At the end of the laboratory period, wrap the frog in a wet paper towel and put it in a plastic bag. Tie the bag closed and label it with your name and your partner's. **CAUTION:** *Wash your hands with soap and water after working with the preserved frog.*

Part B. The Frog's Internal Anatomy

1. Lay the frog on its back in the tray. Wear your safety goggles, laboratory apron, and disposable gloves. Use the dissecting pins to attach the limbs to the wax in the tray. With the forceps, gently lift the loose skin where the frog's hindlimbs meet. Use the scissors to make an incision through the raised skin. Cut the skin as shown in Figure 3, along the center of the body to the base of the head. Then cut the skin laterally from the central incision to each of the limbs. Lift the skin flaps and pin them to the wax in the tray as shown in Figure 4.

2. Cut the muscle of the body wall as you cut the skin. Raise the muscle with your scissors as you cut to avoid damaging the structures underneath. When you reach the forelimbs, you will have to cut through the frog's breastbone, or sternum.

3. Pin back the muscle flaps to expose the internal organs. If the frog is a female, the organs may be covered with a mass of black and white eggs. If so, cut away the eggs and remove them. Yellow fingerlike structures, called fat bodies, may also be covering some organs. Remove those structures as well. Dispose of the eggs and fat bodies according to your teacher's instructions.

Part C. Digestive System

1. Find the large, lobed, reddish-brown organ in the middle of the body cavity. This organ is the liver, which stores food, aids fat digestion by producing a substance called bile, and removes poisonous wastes from the blood.

2. Use the dissecting probe to gently raise the liver. Under the liver you will find a greenish sac called the gall bladder. This organ stores the bile produced by the liver before it passes into the small intestine.

3. The oval, whitish sac is the frog's stomach. The esophagus carries food from the mouth to the stomach where it is partially digested. From the stomach, food passes into the small intestine, where digestion is completed. Find the thin, ribbonlike pancreas lying above the curved end of the stomach. This organ secretes digestive enzymes into the small intestine.

4. Notice that the small intestine is looped. With the dissecting probe, lift the small intestine. Using the forceps, carefully remove some of the connecting tissue that holds the small intestine in place. The small intestine leads to a wider tube called the large intestine. Food wastes pass from the large intestine to the cloaca, a large sac that passes wastes out of the frog's body.

5. Draw and label parts of the frog's digestive system in Figure 6 on page 222.

Part D. Circulatory and Respiratory Systems

1. Find the heart, a reddish triangular organ in the middle of the upper body. The heart has three chambers. The two upper atria collect blood from the veins and pass the blood to the lower chamber, the ventricle. The ventricle pumps the blood throughout the body through arteries.

2. The red, pea-shaped organ near the small intestine is the spleen. It produces white blood cells and removes dead red blood cells from the blood.

3. Locate the pair of spongy-textured lungs on either side of the heart. A frog takes in air through its external nares and enlarges its mouth by lowering the floor of the mouth. Then it closes its external nares and raises the floor of the mouth, forcing air through the glottis into the lungs.

4. Draw and label the heart, spleen, and lungs in Figure 6 on page 222.

Part E. Excretory and Reproductive Systems

1. Gently move the small intestines to the side with a dissecting probe. The two long, dark organs embedded in the back wall are the kidneys. The yellow, fingerlike projections above each kidney are fat bodies, which store fat. The kidneys filter chemical wastes from the blood. Find the tube, called the urinary duct, that leads from each kidney to the urinary bladder. The urinary bladder empties into the cloaca through which the urine, eggs, and sperm are eliminated from the body.

2. If your frog is filled with eggs, it is a female ready for breeding. If your frog is a female not ready for breeding, the egg-producing ovaries appear as thin-walled, gray, folded tissues attached to the kidneys. A coiled white tube, called an oviduct, leads from each ovary and carries eggs to an ovisac where the eggs are stored until a male squeezes the eggs from the female's body.

3. The yellow, bean-shaped testes of a male frog are attached to the kidneys. Sperm from the testes pass through the urinary duct into the cloaca.

4. Draw and label the excretory and reproductive structures of the male or female frog in Figure 7 below.

5. When you have finished your dissections, dispose of the frog as instructed by your teacher. Wash your hands with soap and water.

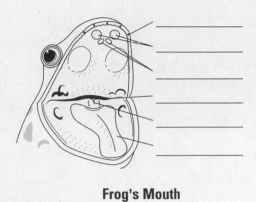

Frog's Mouth

Figure 5

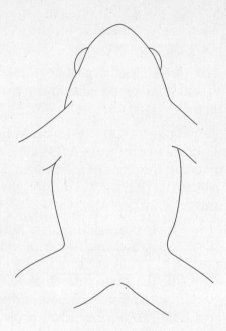

Circulatory, Digestive, and Respiratory Systems

Figure 6

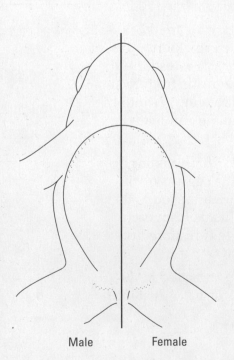

Male   Female

Reproductive and Excretory Systems

Figure 7

Analysis and Conclusions

1. **Drawing Conclusions** Identify three functions of a frog's cloaca.

_____

_____

2. **Inferring** Explain how the length of the small intestine relates to its function in absorbing nutrients.

_____

_____

3. **Drawing Conclusions** Explain how the frog's hindlimbs are adapted for life on land and in water.

_____

_____

_____

4. **Formulating Hypotheses** Describe a situation in which the location of the frog's external nares would be an advantage in breathing.

_____

_____

_____

5. **Inferring** Infer how the attachment of the frog's tongue helps it to catch prey.

_____

_____

_____

6. **Comparing and Contrasting** From your knowledge of the habitat and behavior of frogs and humans, can you deduce which of their internal structures differ? Explain your answer.

_____

_____

_____

Going Further

Based on the results of this investigation, develop a hypothesis about whether or not the internal organs of frogs are similar to the internal organs of other amphibians. Propose an experiment to test your hypothesis. If the necessary resources are available and you have your teacher's permission, perform the experiment.

Examining Adaptations in Lizards

Introduction

Reptiles are ectothermic, or coldblooded vertebrates that are covered with dry scaly skin. They are adapted for reproduction on land. Most species are land-dwelling, but some species spend much time in water. Turtles, snakes, lizards, crocodiles, and alligators are reptiles. Reptilian skin is dry, thick, and waterproof, protecting the body from drying out even in very dry climates. The skin is covered by tough scales that protect the animal from injury.

The anole, or American chameleon, is a common lizard found throughout the southern United States. It can be found on shrubs, trees, and fences, and on the ground. Often it is found around homes, and it seems to thrive in areas inhabited by humans. The anole is best known for the ability of its skin color to change from green to brown or gray. This change in skin color is thought to be stimulated by changes in light intensity, temperature, and emotional state.

In this investigation, you will observe the external structures of an anole. You will also design an experiment to observe its response to environmental change.

Problem

What are the external structures of a lizard? What changes occur in a lizard's coloration in different environments?

Pre-Lab Discussion

Read the entire investigation. Then, work with a partner to answer the following questions.

1. Anoles are found in dry environments. What types of body structures would you predict anoles to have?

   _____

   _____

2. What evidence would indicate that anoles are land-dwelling rather than water-dwelling animals?

   _____

   _____

3. What is the difference between Part A and Part B of this investigation?

   _____

   _____

   _____

4. What kinds of things are easier to examine in a preserved anole than in a live animal? What can you learn from the live animal that you can't learn from the preserved specimen?

_____

_____

_____

5. What is the purpose of averaging the measurements and calculations you will make in Step 2 of Part A of the investigation?

_____

_____

Suggested Materials *(per group)*

preserved anole
live anole
6 sheets of construction paper
  (green, yellow, brown, red, black, and white)
metric ruler
dissecting tray
paper towels

Safety 🔲🔲🔲🔲

Put on plastic gloves and a laboratory apron if one is available. Always use special caution when working with laboratory chemicals, as they may irritate the skin or cause staining of the skin or clothing. Never touch or taste any chemical unless instructed to do so. Follow your teacher's directions and all appropriate safety procedures when handling live animals. Note all safety symbols next to the steps in Design Your Experiment and review the meanings of each symbol by referring to Safety Symbols on page 8.

Design Your Experiment

Part A. External Anatomy of the Anole

1. Obtain a preserved anole. Rinse the anole with water to remove excess preservative. **CAUTION:** *The preservative used on the anole can irritate your skin. Avoid touching your eyes while working with the anole.* Dry the anole with paper towels and place it on a dissecting tray.

2. Measure the entire body length of the anole in centimeters. Record this measurement in Data Table 1. Also measure the length of the tail alone in centimeters. Record this measurement in Data Table 1. Obtain the measurements of four other groups of students and record this information in Data Table 1. Determine the average length of the five anoles and their tails and record this information in Data Table 1.

Data Table 1

Anole	Entire Body Length (cm)	Tail Length Only (cm)
1		
2		
3		
4		
5		
Average		

3. Observe the texture and color of the anole's skin. Answer questions 1 and 2.

4. Indentify the sex of your anole. Males are generally larger than females and have a dewlap, or fold of skin under the neck. Females have only a small, primitive dewlap. Answer question 3 in Analysis and Conclusions.

5. Locate the head, trunk, and tail of the anole.

6. Examine the head of the anole. Look for the presence of eyelids and external ear openings. Look for the presence of nostrils.

7. Open the mouth of the anole. Look for the presence of teeth.

8. Examine the feet of the anole.

9. In Figure 1 label the following external structures of the anole: head, trunk, tail, dewlap, foot, nostrils, and external ear opening.

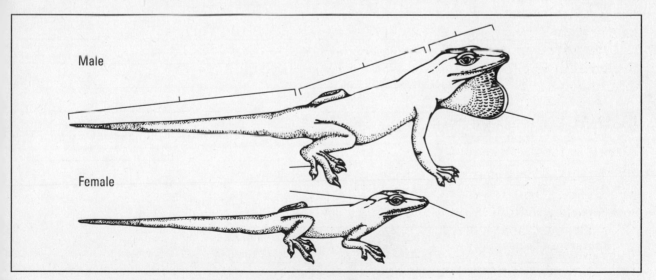

External Anatomy of the Anole

Figure 1

10. Follow your teacher's instructions for storing the anole for further use.

Part B. Your Own Experiment

1. **Formulating Hypotheses** Does an anole change color to adapt to changes in its environment? Record your hypothesis in the space provided.

2. **Designing Experiments** Obtain a live anole. Design an experiment to investigate how an anole responds to changes in the color of its environment. Outline the steps in your procedure in the space provided.

3. Obtain your teacher's approval for your experimental procedure. Then carry out the experiment.

4. Use Data Table 2 to record your observations.

Hypothesis:

_____

_____

_____

Manipulated Variable:

_____

Responding Variable:

_____

Controlled Variable:

_____

Procedure:

_____

_____

_____

_____

_____

_____

_____

_____

Data Table 2

Background Color	Original Color of Anole	Anole Color After Several Minutes

Analysis and Conclusions

1. **Observing** Describe the texture and appearance of the anole's skin.

   _____

   _____

2. **Observing** What is the color of your anole?

   _____

3. **Inferring** What is the sex of your anole? How can you tell?

   _____

   _____

4. **Analyzing Data** How does the anole's average tail length compare to its average body length?

   _____

   _____

   _____

5. **Formulating Hypotheses** What is the possible function of the dewlap?

   _____

   _____

   _____

6. **Inferring** What is the function of the eyelids on the anole?

   _____

   _____

   _____

7. **Inferring** What is the function of the teeth of the anole?

   _____

   _____

8. **Inferring** How are the anole's feet adapted for life on land?

   _____

   _____

9. **Analyzing Data** Review your hypothesis and the observations you recorded in Data Table 2. Use your observations to confirm or reject your hypothesis.

   _____

   _____

   _____

10. Inferring The anole has the ability to lose its tail and then regenerate a new one. How is this a useful adaptation for the anole?

_____

_____

11. Observing Name three adaptations that anoles have for living on land.

_____

_____

Going Further

Obtain a liquid-crystal temperature strip. Under the supervision of your teacher, hold the strip against the skin of a live anole. Record the surface temperature of the anole. Place the anole in the sun for 5 minutes and check the temperature again. Carry out the same procedure with a small mammal such as a gerbil or hamster and compare the results.

Comparing Primates

Introduction

In *The Descent of Man*, the English naturalist Charles Darwin formulated the hypothesis that humans and other primates have a common ancestor. All scientific hypotheses, including this one, are tested by observations. For example, observations of fossils lend support to Darwin's hypothesis of human origins.

Darwin observed that despite common ancestry, human beings and other primates differ in many important ways. Although all primates have opposable thumbs, the human hand is capable of more refined and exact movements than those of other primates. The human braincase, or cranium, has more volume than those of other primates. Human beings are bipedal, or able to walk on two limbs. Other primates use all four limbs for locomotion. Being bipedal frees the arms and hands for other tasks, such as toolmaking. Darwin regarded these human traits as adaptations, resulting from natural selection. The adaptations of other primates, he suggested, evolved differently.

In this investigation, you will examine the skeletal features of different primates in order to understand the evolutionary relationships among them.

Problem

How can skeletal evidence be used to understand the evolutionary relationships of primates?

Pre-Lab Discussion

Read through the entire investigation. Then, work with a partner to answer the following questions.

1. What hypothesis did Charles Darwin formulate about evolutionary relationships of humans and other primates?

   _____

   _____

2. What characteristics of primates will be examined in this investigation?

   _____

   _____

3. How do the hand and cranium of humans differ from those of other primates? Suggest what behaviors these traits might allow?

   _____

   _____

   _____

   _____

4. What does it mean to be bipedal and how might it benefit a primate?

_____

_____

5. What determines the characteristics of organisms like those examined in this investigation?

_____

_____

Materials *(per student)*

metric ruler
protractor

Procedure

1. In Figure 1 measure the length in millimeters of lines *ab* and *bc* the lower jaw of each primate. Record these lengths in Data Table 1. Record the product of these lengths in Data Table 1.

2. Use a protractor to measure the angle *xy* in each primate skull in Figure 1. Record your observations in Data Table 1 on page 234.

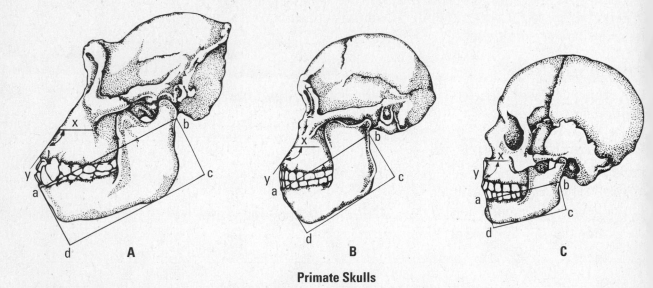

Primate Skulls

Figure 1

3. Examine the teeth of each of the three primates in Figure 2.

4. Count the number of incisors, canines, premolars, and molars of each primate jaw in Figure 2. Record your observations in the appropriate columns in Data Table 2 on page 234.

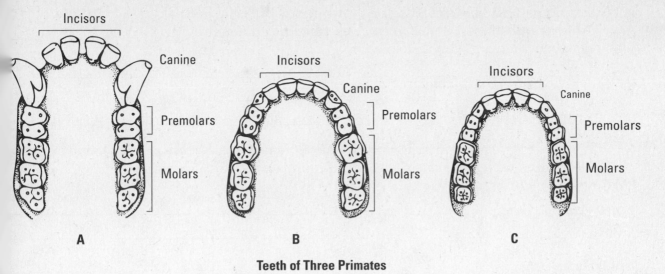

Teeth of Three Primates

Figure 2

5. Examine the two skeletons in Figure 3.

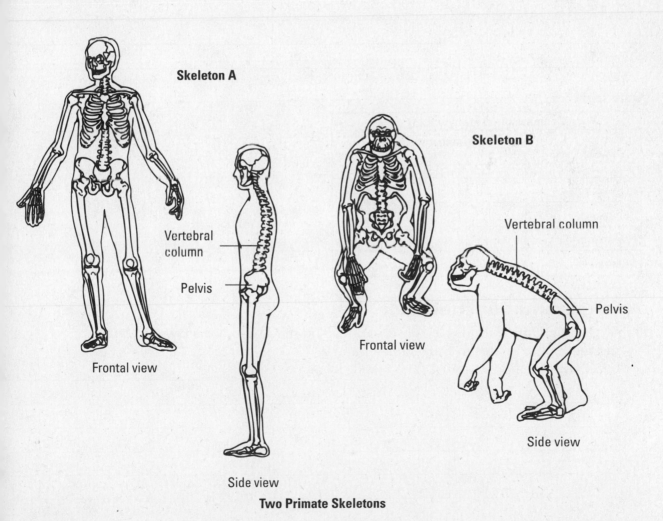

Two Primate Skeletons

Figure 3

6. Compare both views of Skeleton A with those of Skeleton B. Answer questions 1 and 2 below. Describe three differences between Skeleton A and Skeleton B.

_____

_____

_____

_____

7. Determine which primate skeleton in Figure 3 is bipedal. Record your conclusion below.

_____

_____

Data Table 1

	Comparison of Three Primate Skulls			
Skull	Length of Lower Jaw (mm) *(ab)*	Depth of Lower Jaw (mm) *(bc)*	Area of Lower Jaw (mm²) *(ab × bc)*	Angle of Jaw
A				
B				
C				

Data Table 2

Comparison of Primate Teeth			
Type of Teeth	Number of Teeth		
	A	B	C
Incisors			
Canines			
Premolars			
Molars			

Analysis and Conclusions

1. **Analyzing Data** Discuss the observations you made about the jaws and teeth of primates in Data Tables 1 and 2.

_____

_____

_____

_____

_____

_____

2. **Analyzing Data** Discuss the observations you made about the two primate skeletons shown in Figure 3.

_____

_____

_____

_____

3. **Drawing Conclusions** Based upon your observations of Figures 1 and 2, identify primates A to C as gorilla, chimpanzee, or human. Explain your answers.

_____

_____

_____

4. **Drawing Conclusions** Based upon the skulls and teeth, which two primates are most different from one another? Does one primate seem intermediate between the other two?

_____

_____

_____

5. **Drawing Conclusions** Which of the two types of primates shown in Figure 3 is human? What conclusion can be made about its mode of transportation and what would be the benefits of this mode?

_____

_____

_____

6. **Inferring** Based on teeth structure, tell how the diet of primate A might differ from that of primate C?

_____

_____

_____

7. **Evaluating** Do you think the observations you made in this investigation support Darwin's hypothesis? Explain why or why not.

_____

_____

_____

Going Further

Visit a local zoo to observe the behavior of gorillas, chimpanzees, baboons, and other primates. Observe the ways in which the animals communicate and interact with one another. What similarities and differences do you observe between the behaviors of the primates you studied and those of human beings? Use a notebook to record your observations.

Observing Vertebrate Skeletons

Introduction

One characteristic common to all vertebrates is the presence of a skeleton. The endoskeleton provides support, protects the internal organs, and is a site for the attachment of muscles. In jawless fishes—lampreys and hagfishes—and in sharks and rays, the endoskeleton is made of cartilage. Other vertebrates have endoskeletons of bone with small amounts of cartilage present.

Similar skeletal features reveal important evolutionary links among vertebrates. Structures such as bones that have a common origin but different function are called homologous structures.

In this investigation, you will compare the skeletons of several different vertebrates and look for evidence of homologous structures. You will also classify unknown bone specimens based on their similarities to and differences from known vertebrates.

Problem

What homologous structures can be identified in vertebrate skeletons?

Pre-Lab Discussion

Read the entire investigation. Then, work with a partner to answer the following questions.

1. Why isn't every individual bone of the human skeleton labeled?

_____

_____

2. Which labels on the human skeleton show specific groups of bones?

_____

_____

3. How will you label the bones in Figure 3?

_____

_____

4. How will you begin to identify your mystery bones?

_____

_____

5. Are you certain that your mystery bones will be from an animal whose skeleton is pictured in this lab?

_____

_____

Materials *(per group)*

set of "mystery" bones

Procedure

1. Carefully examine the labeled human skeleton in Figure 1. The human skeleton contains more than 200 bones. Become familiar with the names and structures of the bones in Figure 1.

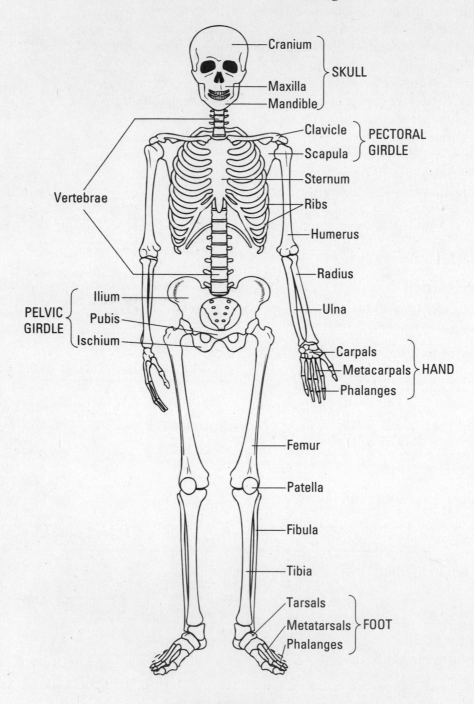

Human Skeleton

Figure 1

2. Look at the frog skeleton in Figure 2. As you examine the skeleton, compare it to the human skeleton in Figure 1. Label the bones of the frog skeleton using the names from Figure 1.

3. Repeat step 2 with the skeletons of the crocodile, pigeon, and cat in Figures 3, 4, and 5.

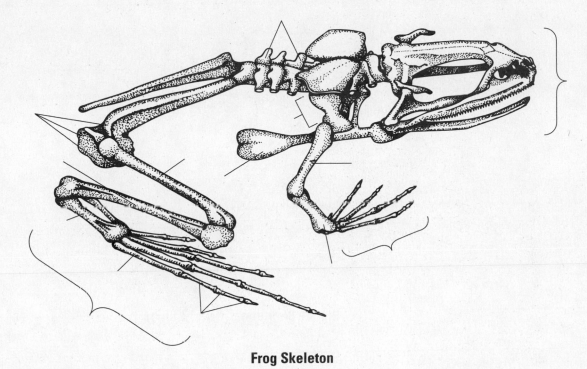

Frog Skeleton

Figure 2

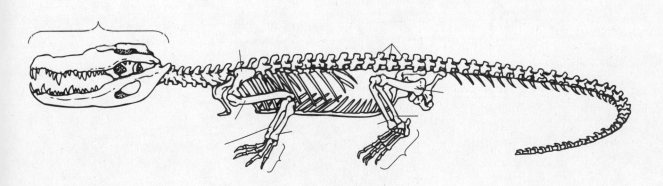

Crocodile Skeleton

Figure 3

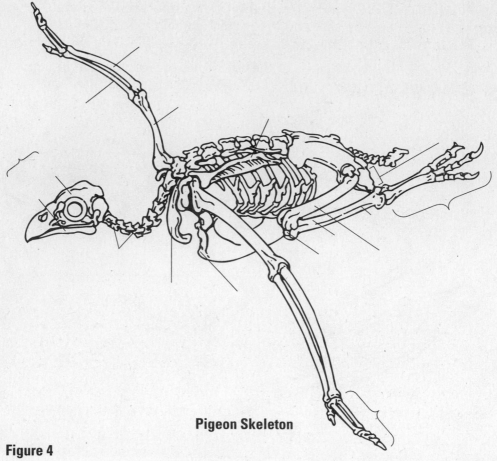

Pigeon Skeleton

Figure 4

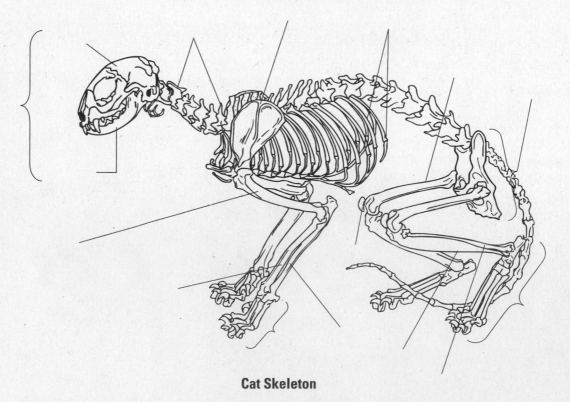

Cat Skeleton

Figure 5

4. Obtain a set of "mystery" bones from your teacher. Identify the bones by comparing them to the bones of each skeleton observed in this investigation. Answer questions 9 and 10 in Analysis and Conclusions.

Analysis and Conclusions

1. Comparing and Contrasting What are three characteristics that all of the skeletons share?

_____

_____

2. Comparing and Contrasting What are three differences that exist among the skeletons?

_____

_____

3. Comparing and Contrasting How are the vertebral columns of the skeletons similar? How are they different?

_____

_____

_____

4. Comparing and Contrasting How are the hindlimbs similar? How are they different?

_____

_____

_____

5. Comparing and Contrasting How do the foot bones of these vertebrates differ from one another?

_____

_____

_____

6. Observing Describe the "mystery" bones in your collection.

_____

_____

7. Classifying To what parts of the skeleton do your "mystery" bones belong?

_____

_____

8. **Inferring** How do the functions of the forelimbs differ among the five vertebrates you have examined?

_____

_____

_____

9. **Analyzing Data** What type of evidence indicates that the human hand, pigeon wing, and cat paw are homologous structures?

_____

_____

10. **Drawing Conclusions** To what type of animal do you think your "mystery" bones belong? On what evidence do you base your conclusion?

_____

_____

_____

11. **Drawing Conclusions** Are bones that are similar in structure always similar in function? Give an example to defend your answer.

_____

_____

_____

_____

12. **Drawing Conclusions** What evidence have you obtained in this investigation to support the theory that vertebrates evolved from a common ancestor?

_____

_____

_____

13. **Drawing Conclusions** Which of the skeletons is most closely related to humans? What evidence supports your answer?

_____

_____

_____

_____

Going Further

Using reference materials, find examples of other vertebrate skeletons. How are these skeletons similar to and different from those you have studied in this investigation? How are the skeletons of these other vertebrates adapted to the environments in which they live?

Chapter 34   Animal Behavior

Observing Animal Behavior

Introduction

The way in which an organism resonds to its environment is called behavior. Behaviors can be classified as either inborn or learned. Inborn behavior is also referred to as involuntary, innate, or instinctive behavior. Inborn behaviors are predictable, automatic responses to physical or psychological stimuli. The simplest inborn behaviors are known as reflexes. Some reflexes coordinate internal body processes, such as the slowing or quickening of the heartbeat. Other reflexes protect the organism. For example, when a cat is frightened by another animal, it will arch its back and fluff up its fur. This response makes the cat appear larger in an attempt to scare away the other animal.

Learned behavior is also referred to as acquired, voluntary, or conditioned behavior. This type of behavior depends on memory, repetition, and experience. Learning gives animals flexibility in the way they respond to situations, allowing them to deal with uncertainty and change. Although it's common to discuss behaviors in terms of being either inborn or learned, most behaviors result from a combination of both innate ability and learning.

In this investigation, you will be observing both inborn and learned behaviors of a small mammal—a rodent.

Problem

What is a behavior? How do inborn and learned behaviors differ?

Pre-Lab Discussion

Read the entire investigation. Then, work with a partner to answer the following questions.

1. List at least three stimuli you expect the rodent to respond to in each part of the investigation.

   _____

   _____

   _____

2. Predict how the two rodents will react when placed in a box together.

   _____

   _____

3. In Part A, what is the purpose of placing the flower pot inside a larger box before placing the rodent in it?

   _____

   _____

   _____

4. Do you think the amount of time it takes the rodent to complete the maze in Part B will increase or decrease over the five trials? Explain your answer.

_____

_____

_____

_____

5. What types of behavior—inborn or learned—do you think Parts A and B of the Procedure are intended to reveal? Explain your answers.

_____

_____

_____

_____

Materials *(per group)*

rodent
thick gloves
small animal cage or cardboard box
clay flower pot, 10 cm high
box or other large container
animal maze
clock or watch with second hand

Safety 🖼🧤🔬🐁

Put on a laboratory apron if one is available. Be careful to avoid breakage when working with the clay flower pot. Follow your teacher's directions and all appropriate safety procedures when handling live animals. Wash your hands thoroughly after carrying out this investigation. Note all safety alert symbols next to the steps in the Procedure and review the meanings of each symbol by referring to Safety Symbols on page 8.

Procedure

Part A. Observing a Rodent in Different Environments

1. Obtain a rodent in a container from your teacher. Observe the physical characteristics of your rodent. Answer the questions below. **CAUTION:** *Put on a laboratory apron and thick, leather gloves before handling the rodent. Follow your teacher's directions and all appropriate safety procedures while working with the rodent.*

2. Observe any behavioral responses of the rodent as it moves around its cage or box. Record your observations in Data Table 1.

3. Working with another group of students, carefully pick up your rodent and place it in the box of another rodent of the same species. Observe the two rodents' behaviors as they interact with each other. Record your observations in Data Table 1. **CAUTION:** *Handle the animals carefully and gently, without frightening them. Mice and rats may be picked up gently by their tails. Do not pick up gerbils or hamsters by their tails because the tips of their tails will break off. Separate the animals immediately if one attacks the other.*

4. Return your rodent to its cage or box and allow it to readjust to its surroundings for several minutes.

5. Place an empty clay flower pot in a larger box or other container. Gently pick up your rodent and place it in the clay flower pot with slanted sides, as shown in Figure 1. Observe the rodent as it explores the flower pot, and record your observations in Data Table 1. Record the time it takes the rodent to explore the flower pot, seek a way out and escape. Record the number of times it attempts to escape before succeeding. **CAUTION:** *The clay pot can break and cut you. Handle it carefully and notify your teacher immediately of any breakages. Do not clean up broken pots unless you teacher instructs you to do so.*

Rodent

Flower pot

Figure 1

6. Return the rodent to its original cage or box and allow it to readjust to its surroundings for several minutes before beginning Part B.

Part B. Observing a Rodent's Run Through a Maze

1. Obtain a maze from your teacher. Place a piece of rodent food at the end of the maze. Carefully place the rodent at the beginning of the maze, as shown in Figure 2.

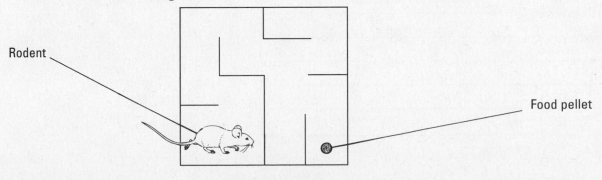

Rodent

Food pellet

Figure 2   **Top View of Animal Maze**

2. In Data Table 2, record the time it takes the rodent to successfully complete the maze the first time.

3. Repeat steps 1 and 2 four more times and record the times in Data Table 2.

4. Return the rodent to its original cage or box. Return the rodent to your teacher. **CAUTION:** *Wash your hands thoroughly after completing this investigation.*

Data Table 1

Type of Environment	Animal Behaviors
Alone in a large area	
In an area with another member of the same species	
Alone in small, confining area	

Data Table 2

Trial	Time Needed to Complete Maze
1	
2	
3	
4	
5	

Analysis and Conclusions

1. **Observing** In what ways did your rodent's behavior change when it came in contact with another rodent after having been alone?

_____

_____

_____

2. **Inferring** Why might an animal's behavior change when it comes in contact with another animal of its own species?

_____

_____

_____

3. **Observing** In what ways did your rodent's behavior change when it was placed in a small, confining place?

_____

_____

_____

4. **Inferring** Why might an animal respond differently to a small confining area than to a large nonconfining area?

_____

_____

_____

5. **Comparing and Contrasting** How did the time it took the rodent to run the maze the first time compare with the time it took the rodent to run it the fifth time? Why might a change in time have occurred?

_____

_____

_____

6. **Classifying** How would you classify the behaviors you recorded in each data table—as inborn or learned? Explain your classifications.

_____

_____

_____

_____

_____

Going Further

Due to the incredible variety of physical and behavioral adaptations they possess, insects have been successful in inhabiting even the harshest and remotest places on Earth. To observe the complex behaviors of ants, cut off the top of a 2-liter clear plastic soft drink bottle. Fill an individual-sized soft drink bottle with water and place it inside the 2-liter bottle. Fill the space between the two bottles with moistened sandy soil. Place a 10-centimeter-long piece of cotton in the small bottle to serve as a wick to provide water for the ants. Have your teacher place about a dozen ants on the sand. To cover the outside of the 2-liter soft drink bottle, wrap a piece of plastic wrap over the opening and tape it to the sides of the bottle. Use a straight pin to make about 10 small holes in the plastic wrap. Place the entire setup in a pan of shallow water to keep the ants from escaping. Wash your hands thoroughly after setting up your ant container and after each feeding and observation. Place food on the surface of the soil three times a week. Small pieces of lettuce and hard-boiled egg yolks make good ant food. Using a hand lens, observe the ants twice a week for one month. Use a notebook to record any social behaviors you observe among members of the ant colony. **CAUTION:** *Do not handle the insects if you are allergic to their stings. Wear protective gloves when handling insects. Follow your teacher's directions and all appropriate safety procedures when working with live animals. Be careful when handling the scissors and cutting the plastic bottle. Point the scissors away from your body at all times. The cut edge of the plastic bottle can cut your skin.*

Observing Nervous Responses

Introduction

The nervous system is a series of conducting tissues that carries impulses to all parts of the body. Your nervous system initiates many types of reflex actions. When you touch a hot object, you immediately pull your hand away. You might be aware of this reflex action occurring, but you are unable to stop or control it.

How do reflex actions occur? When your hand touches a hot object, for example, heat receptors in the skin send an impulse to the muscles of the arm to contract. The impulse travels along the sensory neurons, to the spinal cord, across a synapse, and stimulates a motor neuron. The impulse leaves the spinal cord, passes back to the same nerve, and back to the arm muscles, causing them to contract and pull your hand away. This pathway is called the reflex arc. Because the reflex arc involves only the spinal cord and not the brain, a reflex action occurs in a matter of a fraction of a second. you are not able to control a reflex—it happens automatically.

In a nonreflex response, an impulse must travel to the brain. The brain interprets the stimulus and initiates an appropriate response. In this case, the time it takes to respond is measurably longer than the time required for a reflex arc. A person's reaction time can be measured by how quickly he or she can perceive a stimulus and then react to it. Driving a car and playing tennis are examples of activities in which reaction time is very important.

In this investigation, you will observe two reflex actions and measure your reaction time.

Problem

Can you control reflex actions? How can you measure reaction time?

Pre-Lab Discussion

Read the entire investigation. Then, work with a partner to answer the following questions.

1. What data will you record in Data Table 2?

_____

_____

2. What is another name for an involuntary or automatic response to a stimulus?

_____

3. What caution should you observe for shining the light?

_____

_____

4. Why do you put your elbow on the table when you are catching the meterstick?

_____

_____

5. In Part A, why do you use an eyepatch instead of just closing your eye?

_____

_____

Materials _(per group)_

pen light
eye patch or eye cover
meterstick

Safety 🖐

This experiment involves physical contact. Avoid this experiment if a problem with the knee, eye, or hand exists. Note the safety alert symbol next to step 3 in the Procedure and review the meaning of the symbol by referring to Safety Symbols on page 8.

Procedure

Part A. Reflexes

1. Sit on a chair or stool.

2. Cross your left leg over your right.

🖐 3. Have a member of your group tap your knee firmly, slightly below the knee cap, with the side of his or her hand, as shown in Figure 1. **CAUTION:** _Be sure the knee is not hit hard. A firm, quick tap is sufficient. Avoid this experiment if a physical problem in the knee exists._ Record your observations.

Figure 1

4. Repeat steps 1 to 3. This time, try to stop your knee from jerking. Record your observations.

5. Reverse roles and repeat steps 1 to 4.

6. Sit on a chair or stool.

7. Close one eye and cover it with the eye patch. Keep the other eye open.

8. Have a group member shine the pen light close to the open eye for about 10 seconds. **CAUTION:** *Do not shine light directly into the eye.*

9. Quickly remove the patch from the other eye.

10. Have a group member observe what happens to the pupils of both the eye exposed to light and the eye that remained in darkness. Record the observations in Data Table 1.

Data Table 1

Stimulus	Observations
Light	
Dark	

11. Reversing your roles, repeat steps 6 to 10.

Part B. Reaction Time

1. Rest your elbow on a table and extend your arm over its side as shown in Figure 2.

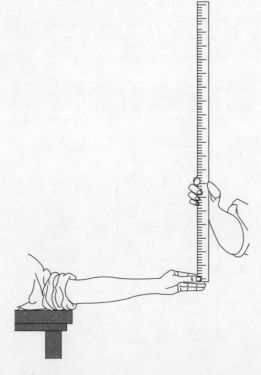

Figure 2

2. Have a group member hold a meterstick in the air, with the 0-cm line between the thumb and index finger of your extended hand.

3. Have the group member drop the meterstick without advance notice. Try to catch it between your thumb and index finger as quickly as possible.

4. In Data Table 2, record in centimeters the position of your thumb and index finger. This is the distance the meterstick fell before you caught it.

5. Repeat steps 2 to 4 three times.

Data Table 2

Trial	Distance (cm)
1	
2	
3	
4	

Analysis and Conclusions

1. **Observing** What happened to your knee when it was tapped?

_____

_____

2. **Inferring** Could you prevent the knee jerk or the pupil contraction? Explain your answer.

_____

_____

3. **Observing** What happened to the pupil of the eye that was close to the light?

_____

4. **Inferring** How does the amount of light affect the pupils?

_____

_____

5. **Classifying** Is catching the meterstick a voluntary reaction or a reflex? Explain your answer.

_____

_____

6. **Calculating** What was the average distance the meterstick fell in your four trials?

_____

_____

7. Comparing and Contrasting In catching the meterstick, were your reactions faster or slower than those of your classmates? How do you know?

_____

_____

_____

8. Classifying From your observations, how would you classify the knee-jerk and the pupillary response? Explain your reason.

_____

_____

9. Drawing Conclusions Suggest some possible ways that reflex arcs could be advantageous to a species.

_____

_____

_____

_____

Going Further

Do the senses of sight, smell, hearing, taste, and touch also affect our reflex actions? Why does your mouth water when you are hungry and see a picture of a delicious meal? Ivan Pavlov, a Russian biologist, carried out many experiments on conditioned reflexes. What are conditioned reflexes? How are stimulus and response related? Use resources in your school library or on the Internet to find out more about conditioned reflexes. Share your findings with the class.

Observing Bone Composition and Structure

Introduction

Human bone contains living tissue and nonliving materials. The living tissue includes bone cells, blood vessels, fat cells, nerve cells, and cartilage cells. The nonliving materials include water, extra cells, protein, and minerals, such as calcium and phosphorus. In fact, bones are hard and strong because they contain a great amount of calcium. Bone is composed of compact bone and spongy bone. Unlike compact bone, which is very hard and dense, spongy bone is soft and has many spaces in it.

In this investigation, you will examine the internal structure of compact bone. You will also determine the percentage of water in bone and observe how calcium gives strength to bone.

Problem

What is the internal composition and structure of bone?

Pre-Lab Discussion

Read the entire investigation. Then, work with a partner to answer the following questions.

1. What is the purpose of heating the bone in Part A?

_____

_____

2. Why do you find the mass of the bone before you heat it?

_____

_____

3. What should you do while your bone is in the oven for 25 minutes?

_____

_____

4. Predict what will happen to the bone after it soaks in hydrochloric acid for several days.

_____

_____

_____

5. Predict the properties of a bone that is low in calcium.

_____

_____

Materials *(per group)*

prepared slide of compact bone
  with Haversian system

microscope

2 uncooked pork or beef bones

triple-beam balance

marker

heat-resistant gloves

heat-resistant pad

large metal cookie sheet or cooking tray

100 mL of 20% hydrochloric
  acid solution

250-mL beaker

oven

tongs

paper towels

100-mL graduated cylinder

masking tape

nitrile gloves

Safety

Put on a laboratory apron if one is available. Put on safety goggles. Be careful to avoid breakage when working with glassware. Observe proper laboratory procedures when using electrical equipment. Use extreme care when working with heated equipment and materials to avoid burns. Always use special caution when working with laboratory chemicals, as they may irritate the skin or stain skin or clothing. Never touch or taste any chemical unless intructed to do so. Always handle the microscope with extreme care. You are responsible for its proper care and use. Use caution when handling glass slides as they can break easily and cut you. Note all safety alert symbols next to the steps in the Procedure and review the meanings of each symbol by referring to Safety Symbols on page 8.

Procedure

Part A. Calculating the Percentage of Water in a Bone

1. Place a small piece of paper towel on the pan of a triple-beam balance. Move the rider on the front beam of the balance until the pointer of the balance points to zero. Find the mass of the paper towel to the nearest tenth of a gram. **CAUTION:** *Put on a laboratory apron before beginning this investigation.*

2. Place the uncooked bone on the balance and find the mass of the bone and paper towel to the nearest tenth of a gram. To determine the mass of the bone, subtract the mass of the paper towel from the mass of the bone and paper towel. Record this information in Data Table 1.

3. Using the marker, write the last name of one of your group members on the surface of the bone.

4. Place the bone, along with bones of the other groups, on a large metal cooking tray. Place the cooking tray in an oven that has been preheated to 149°C (300°F) for 25 minutes. **CAUTION:** *Wear heat-resistant gloves when handling hot materials. Place the tray in the oven carefully to avoid burns.*

5. **CAUTION:** *To avoid burns, use heat-resistant gloves to remove the hot tray from the oven slowly and carefully.* Using heat-resistant gloves, remove the tray from the oven and place it on a heat-resistant pad to cool.

6. After the bone has cooled for 10 minutes, place it on the piece of paper towel on the triple-beam balance and again determine its mass to the nearest tenth of a gram. Record this information in Data Table 1.

Data Table 1

Object	Mass Before Heating (g)	Mass After Heating (g)
Bone		

Percentage of water in bone 5 _____

7. The loss in mass of the bone is due primarily to the evaporation of water and to some oxidation of the minerals in the bone. Calculate the percentage of water in the bone by using the following formula:

$$\frac{\text{mass before heating/mass after heating}}{\text{mass before heating}} \times 100 = \text{percentage of water}$$

8. Record the percentage of water in the bone below Data Table 1.

9. Follow your teacher's instructions for proper disposal of the bone. Wash your hands thoroughly after completing Part A of this investigation.

Part B. Observing Bone Cells

1. Observe a prepared slide of compact bone under the low-power objective of a microscope. Notice the circular-patterned units in the cross section of the bone. Each of these circular units is a Haversian system. **CAUTION:** *Microscope slides have sharp edges and can break. Always handle the microscope with extreme care. Do not use electrical equipment near water or with wet hands. Never use direct sunlight as the light source for a microscope.*

2. Switch to high-power to observe the structures that make up each Haversian system. **Note:** *When switching to the high-power objective, always look at the objective from the side of the microscope so that the objective does not hit or damage the slide.*

3. Focus on a group of concentric circles. The central, hollow core of these circles is called the Haversian canal. The Haversian canal contains nerves and blood vessels. The rings around the Haversian canal are called lamellae (singular, lamella). The small dark cavities between adjacent lamellae are called lacunae (singular, lacuna). Lacunae appear as long, dark areas between lamellae.

4. Within each Haversian system, the lacunae are interconnected by small, branching canals called canaliculi (singular, canaliculus). Canaliculi appear as thin, dark lines that resemble the spokes of a wheel. Fluids pass from one part of the bone to another through the canaliculi.

5. Look for darkly stained bodies within the lacunae. These are the osteocytes, or living bone cells. See Figure 1. Notice that osteocytes have fine branches that extend into the canaliculi. The osteocytes are responsible for controlling the life functions of the bone.

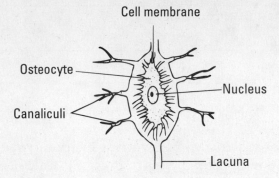

Figure 1

6. In the space provided below, draw a section of bone tissue as seen through the high-power objective of the microscope. Label the following parts of the Haversian system: Haversian canal, lamella, lacuna, canaliculus, and osteocyte. Record the magnification of the microscope.

Magnification _____

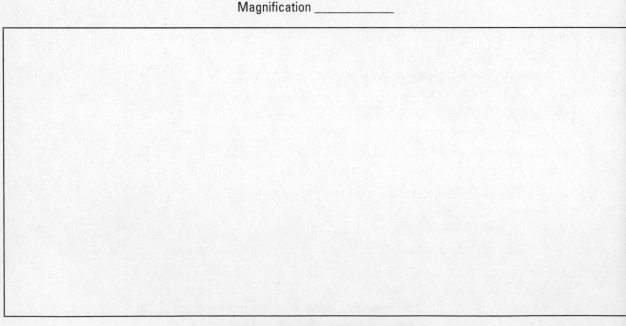

Haversian System of a Human Bone

Part C. Determining the Role of Calcium in a Bone

1. Obtain another uncooked bone. Observe the flexibility of the bone by trying to bend and twist it. Record your observations in Data Table 2.

Data Table 2

Object	Description of Flexibility
Bone before being soaked in acid	
Bone after being soaked in acid	

2. Place the bone in a 250-mL beaker. Use masking tape to label the beaker with the name of one member of your group.

3. Carefully add 100 mL of a 20% hydrochloric acid solution to the beaker. **CAUTION:** *Wear safety goggles and nitrile gloves when using hydrochloric acid. Hydrochloric acid can burn the skin or clothing. If any acid spills on your skin or clothing, wash the affected area with water immediately. Notify your teacher.*

4. Cover the beaker with parafilm or a glass plate. Then label the beaker and place it in a ventilated hood for 3–7 days until the bone becomes spongy. **CAUTION:** *Avoid inhaling the fumes of the acid.*

5. Using tongs, carefully remove the bone from the acid. Rinse the bone under running tap water to remove any acid solution.

6. Dry the bone with a paper towel. Again test the flexibility of the bone. Record your observations in Data Table 2. **CAUTION:** *Do not touch the bone with your bare hands. Wear protective gloves while handling the bone.*

7. Follow your teacher's instructions for the proper disposal of the bone and the acid solution. Wash your hands thoroughly after completing this investigation.

Analysis and Conclusions

1. **Analyzing Data** Is the percentage of water loss in your group's bone exactly the same as that of other groups? If not, why might the percentages vary?

_____

_____

2. **Inferring** Why is water a necessary substance in a bone?

_____

_____

3. **Comparing and Contrasting** Many people incorrectly think of bone as nonliving tissue. How is a bone similar to other living tissues?

_____

_____

_____

4. **Drawing Conclusions** What materials are removed from a bone when it is soaked in a hydrochloric acid solution for several days? What evidence do you have to support your answer?

_____

_____

_____

Going Further

Use reference materials to research the degenerative bone disease known as osteoporosis. What is the cause of this disease? What are its symptoms? What age group does it normally affect? What preventive measures can be taken to combat osteoporosis?

Measuring Lung Capacity

Introduction

The amount of air that you move in and out of your lungs depends on how quickly you are breathing. The amount of air that is moved in and out of the lungs when a person is breathing normally is called the tidal volume. This amount of air provides enough oxygen for the body when the person is resting. It is possible to inhale more deeply and exhale more forcefully than usual. The maximum amount of air moved in and out of the lungs when the deepest possible inspiration is followed by the strongest possible expiration is called the vital capacity.

In this investigation, you will determine the tidal volume and vital capacity of your lungs.

Problem

How are the tidal volume and vital capacity of the human lungs measured?

Pre-Lab Discussion

Read the entire investigation. Then, work with a partner to answer the following questions.

1. Why is it important to measure tidal volume and tidal capacity more than once and then calculate means for these measurements?

_____

_____

2. What would you conclude if the balloon were smaller during your vital capacity measurement than during your tidal volume measurement?

_____

_____

3. List some possible sources of error that could occur during this experiment.

_____

_____

_____

4. How do you expect your estimated vital capacity to compare to your measured vital capacity? Explain your answer.

_____

_____

_____

5. Why might a doctor want to determine the tidal volume or vital capacity of a patient?

_____

_____

_____

Materials _(per pair)_

2 round balloons (1 for each student in the pair)
metric ruler
meterstick
bathroom scale (1 per class is adequate)

Safety 🖾

Do not participate in this investigation if you are ill or if you have any breathing difficulties. You will be exercising during this investigation. If at any time you feel faint or dizzy, sit down and immediately call your teacher. Note the safety alert symbol next in the Procedure and review the meaning of the symbol by referring to Safety Symbols on page 8.

Procedure

Part A. Measuring Tidal Volume

1. Stretch a round balloon lengthwise several times.

2. Inhale normally and then exhale normally into the balloon.
   Note: _Do not force your breathing._

3. Immediately pinch the end of the balloon shut so that no air escapes. Place the balloon on a flat surface. Have your partner use the metric ruler to measure the diameter of the balloon at its widest point, as shown in Figure 1. Record this measurement in Data Table 1.

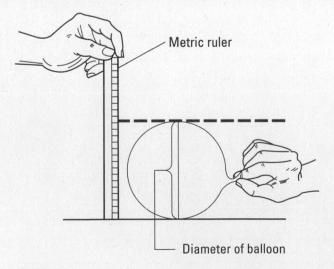
Metric ruler

Diameter of balloon

Figure 1

4. Deflate the balloon and repeat steps 2 and 3 two more times. Use your three measurements to calculate a mean diameter. Record this number in Data Table 1.

Part B. Measuring Vital Capacity

1. After breathing normally, inhale as much air into your lungs as possible. Exhale as much air as you can from your lungs into the balloon.

2. Immediately pinch the end of the balloon shut so that no air escapes. Place the balloon on a flat surface. Have your partner use the metric ruler to measure the diameter of the balloon at its widest point. Record this measurement in Data Table 1.

3. Deflate the balloon and repeat steps 1 and 2 two more times. Use your three measurements to calculate a mean diameter. Record this number in Data Table 1.

4. Use Figure 2 to convert the balloon diameters in Data Table 1 into lung volumes. On the horizontal (x) axis, locate the diameter of the balloon in centimeters and follow the number up until it meets the curved line. Then move across in a straight line to the vertical (y) axis and approximate the lung volume. Record this number in Data Table 2. Repeat this procedure for all of the balloon diameters in Data Table 1.

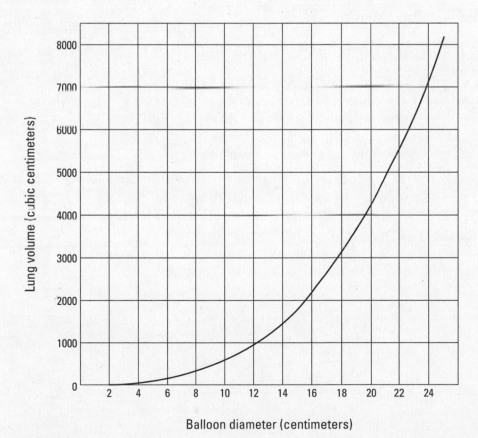

Figure 2

Data Table 1

Balloon Diameter (cm)		
Trial	Tidal Volume	Vital Capacity
1		
2		
3		
Mean		

Data Table 2

Lung Volume (cm³)		
Trial	Tidal Volume	Vital Capacity
1		
2		
3		
Mean		

Part C. Calculating Estimated Vital Capacity

1. Research has shown that the capacity of a person's lungs is proportional to the surface area of his or her body. To find the surface area of your body, you will need to know your height in centimeters and your mass in kilograms. Use a meterstick to find your height and the bathroom scale to find your mass.

2. Use Figure 3 to estimate the surface area of your body. Find your height in centimeters on the left scale. Find your mass in kilograms on the right scale. Lay a metric ruler across Figure 3 so that its edge connects these two points. Now look at the center scale. The point at which the ruler crosses this scale gives your surface area in square meters. Record this number in the space provided on page 265.

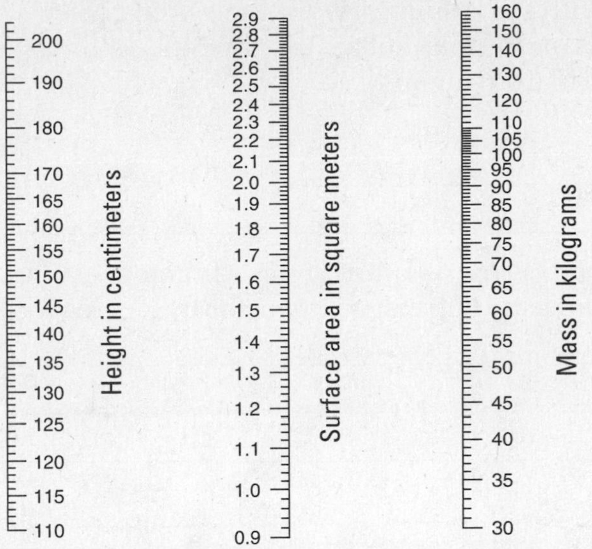

Figure 3

3. To calculate the estimated vital capacity of your lungs, multiply your surface area by the ratio of vital capacity to surface area. For females this ratio is 2000 mL per square meter. For males this ratio is 2500 mL per square meter. Record the estimated vital capacity of your lungs in the space provided below.

Body surface area (m²) _____

Vital capacity (cm³) _____

Analysis and Conclusions

1. **Analyzing Data** How do your tidal volume and vital capacity compare with those of other class members? Why might there be variation among different people?

_____

_____

_____

2. **Comparing and Contrasting** How does your estimated vital capacity compare to your measured vital capacity? Was your prediction in Pre-Lab Discussion question 4 confirmed?

_____

_____

_____

3. **Formulating Hypotheses** If a person forcibly exhales and then relaxes but does not deliberately inhale, air is taken into the lungs. Suggest a hypothesis to explain this phenomenon.

_____

_____

_____

4. **Predicting** A person with the respiratory disease asthma has difficulty exhaling a normal amount of air. How would asthma affect vital capacity? Explain your answer.

_____

_____

_____

5. **Inferring** Aerobic exercise, such as running or swimming, can result in an increase of vital capacity. Suggest a reason for this increase.

_____

_____

_____

Going Further

The vital capacity of the lungs is affected by the anatomical build of a person, the position of the person during the vital capacity measurement, and the stretching capability of the lungs and chest cavity. Measure the vital capacity of your lungs while sitting up and then while lying down. In each position, inhale as much air into your lungs as possible and exhale as much air as you can into a balloon. Measure the diameter of the balloon each time. Compare your vital capacity in each position. Suggest an explanation for any difference between the two volumes.

Simulating Urinalysis

Introduction

All organisms produce wastes that must be removed. In humans, urine is the fluid produced by our kidneys as they remove waste chemicals from the blood. Urine is a watery fluid containing excess salts, nitrogenous wastes, and a variety of organic molecules. The concentration of each of these substances depends on a person's health and diet.

Physicians can evaluate the general health of an individual by testing the chemical composition of urine. Ions such as phosphate and chloride are normally found in urine, but glucose molecules are a symptom of diabetes. Albumin, a protein, is sometimes found in urine after heavy exercise, but the presence of albumin over an extended period can be a symptom of a kidney infection. The analysis of a urine sample is called urinalysis and includes a physical, chemical, and visual examination.

In this investigation you will be testing *artificial* urine samples for the presence of some commonly found chemicals in healthy patients and those with certain diseases.

Problem

Which chemicals are found in the urine of a healthy person and which chemicals can be symptoms of disease?

Pre-Lab Discussion

Read the entire investigation. Then, work with a partner to answer the following questions.

1. In each analysis two samples are tested, one with the chemical and one without it. What is the purpose of testing a sample without the chemical?

   _____

   _____

   _____

2. Which of the tests require heating of the reagent with the sample in a water bath?

   _____

3. Which of the tests require heating of the sample before addition of any reagents?

   _____

4. What substance is detected by reaction with Benedict's solution?

   _____

5. When is the silver nitrate reagent used?

   _____

6. Why is it important to use clean glassware in urinalysis procedures?

_____

Materials *(per group)*

12 test tubes	10% acetic acid solution
glass-marking pencil	simulated urine samples:
test-tube rack	with glucose
test-tube holder	without glucose
10-mL graduated cylinder	with phosphate
hot plate	without phosphate
Bunsen burner	with albumin
400-mL beaker	without albumin
matches	with chloride
Benedict's solution	without chloride
silver nitrate solution	unknown

Safety ☝🏭🧤🥽🖐⚗️🔥🧪☠️🔥👐

Put on safety goggles and put on a laboratory apron if one is available. Observe proper laboratory procedures when using electrical equipment. Be careful using matches. Tie back loose hair and clothing when working with flames and do not reach over an open flame. Always use special caution when working with laboratory chemicals, as they may irritate the skin or stain skin or clothing. Never touch or taste any chemical unless instructed to do so. Wash your hands thoroughly after carrying out this lab. Note all safety alert symbols next to the steps in the Procedure and review the meaning of each symbol by referring to Safety Symbols on page 8.

Procedure

Part A. Test for Glucose

1. Place two test tubes in a test-tube rack. With a glass-marking pencil, label one test tube "G" for glucose. Allow the other test tube to remain unlabeled as it will serve as the control.

2. Use the 400-mL beaker to prepare a hot-water bath. **CAUTION:** *Use extreme care when working with hot water. Do not let the water splash onto your body.*

3. Add 3 mL of Benedict's solution to each test tube. **CAUTION:** *Use extreme care when handling Benedict's solution to avoid staining of the skin and clothing.*

4. Add 3 mL of the simulated urine sample with glucose to the test tube labeled "G." Add 3 mL of the simulated urine sample without glucose to the unlabeled test tube. Note the appearance of the solution in each test tube. Record this information in Data Table 1.

5. Place both test tubes in the hot-water bath for 2 minutes.

6. After 2 minutes, remove the test tubes from the hot-water bath with a test-tube holder. Place the test tubes in the test-tube rack. **CAUTION:** *Be careful when working with heated equipment or materials to avoid burns.* Note any color changes in the test tubes. Record your observations in Data Table 1.

Data Table 1

Substance	Appearance Before Heating	Appearance After Heating
Sample with glucose		
Sample without glucose		

Part B. Test for Chloride

1. Place two test tubes in a test-tube rack. With a glass-marking pencil, label one test tube "C" for chloride. Allow the other test tube to remain unlabeled as it will serve as the control.

2. Add 5 mL of the simulated urine sample with chloride to the test tube labeled "C." Add 5 mL of the urine sample without chloride to the unlabeled test tube. Note the appearance of the substance in each test tube. Record this information in Data Table 2.

3. Carefully add 3 drops of silver nitrate solution to each test tube. **CAUTION:** *Use extreme care when working with silver nitrate solution to avoid staining of the skin and clothing.* Observe the top surface of the liquid in each test tube. Record its appearance in Data Table 2.

Data Table 2

Substance	Appearance Before Adding Silver Nitrate	Appearance After Adding Silver Nitrate
Sample with chloride		
Sample without chloride		

Part C. Test for Albumin

1. Place two test tubes in a test-tube rack. With a glass-marking pencil, label one test tube "A" for albumin. Allow the other test tube to remain unlabeled as it will serve as the control.

2. Half fill the test tube labeled "A" with the simulated urine sample with albumin. Half fill the unlabeled test tube with the simulated urine sample without albumin.

3. Using a test-tube holder, pass the top surface of each test tube over the flame of a Bunsen burner for 15 to 20 seconds, as shown in Figure 1. **CAUTION:** *Secure all loose clothing and hair when using a Bunsen burner. When heating a test tube, always point it away from yourself and other students. Keep your hand to the side of the flame, never above it.* After heating each test tube, place it in a test-tube rack. Note the appearance of each substance. Record your observations in Data Table 3.

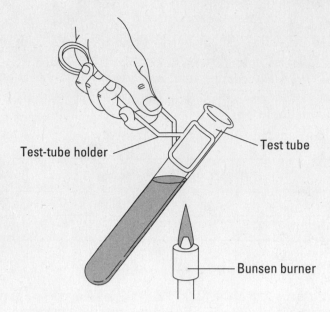

Test-tube holder

Test tube

Bunsen burner

Figure 1

4. Add 5 drops of acetic acid to each test tube. **CAUTION:** *Be careful when using an acid.* Note the appearance of each substance. Record your observations in Data Table 3.

Data Table 3

Substance	Appearance After Heating	Appearance After Adding Acetic Acid
Sample with albumin		
Sample without albumin		

Part D. Test for Phosphate

1. Place two test tubes in a test-tube rack. With a glass-marking pencil, label one test tube "P" for phosphate. Allow the other test tube to remain unlabeled as it will serve as the control.

2. Half fill the test tube labeled "P" with the simulated urine sample with phosphate. Half fill the unlabeled test tube with the simulated urine sample without phosphate.

⚠ 3. Using a test-tube holder, pass the top surface of each test tube over the flame of a Bunsen burner for 15 to 20 seconds. **CAUTION:** *Secure all loose clothing and hair when using a Bunsen burner. When heating a test tube, always point it away from yourself and other students.* After heating each test tube, place it in a test-tube rack. Note the appearance of each substance. Record this information in Data Table 4.

4. Add 5 drops of acetic acid to each test tube. Record your observations in Data Table 4. **CAUTION:** *Be careful when using an acid.*

Data Table 4

Substance	Appearance After Heating	Appearance After Adding Acetic Acid
Sample with phosphate		
Sample without phosphate		

Part E. Testing an Unknown Simulated Urine Sample

1. Obtain a sample of simulated urine marked "unknown." Record the identification number of the sample in Data Table 5.

2. Using four clean test tubes, perform the glucose, chloride, albumin, and phosphate tests on the unknown sample. Follow the Procedures in Parts A through D of this investigation.

3. Record your results in Data Table 5.

Data Table 5

	Composition of Unknown Simulated Urine Sample # _____
Test	**Present or Absent?**
Glucose	
Chloride	
Albumin	
Phosphate	

Analysis and Conclusions

1. **Inferring** Should you always assume that a color change in the urine is a sign of an abnormal condition?

_____

2. **Analyzing Data** Which of the four chemicals tested were found in the unknown sample you analyzed?

_____

3. **Comparing and Contrasting** Which tests should be positive for a normal healthy person?

_____

4. **Predicting** Would it be possible to estimate the amount of a chemical present in a sample based on the strength of the color change?

_____

Going Further

Athletes participating in collegiate competitions are routinely tested for drugs by urinalysis. Use the National Collegiate Athletic Association guidelines to determine which drugs they test for and investigate the tests and their reliability.

Comparing Ovaries and Testes

Introduction

Reproduction is the process by which offspring are produced. The most important function of reproduction is to continue the species. Reproduction may also serve to increase the number of individuals in a species.

Humans reproduce sexually. Gametes are produced in specialized sex organs, or gonads. The gonad of the human male is the testis (plural, testes). The two functions of this organ are the production of sperm cells, which are the male gametes, and the production of the male hormone testosterone. The gonad of the human female is the ovary. The two ovaries of the human female produce egg cells, which are the female gametes, and also secrete female sex hormones.

In this investigation, you will examine prepared slides of mammalian ovaries and testes. You will also investigate the process of egg and sperm production.

Problem

What structures are found in a mammalian ovary and testis? How are eggs and sperm produced?

Pre-Lab Discussion

Read the entire investigation. Then, work with a partner to answer the following questions.

1. In Part A, why should the cross section of the ovary be taken from a nonpregnant cat?

_____

_____

_____

2. Where would you look to find the female hormone estrogen?

_____

_____

3. What care should be taken when switching the microscope from the low power objective to the high power objective?

_____

_____

4. You may observe something stained red on the slide in Part B. What does the red stain most likely indicate?

_____

_____

5. What cells provide nutrients for developing sperm cells?

_____

_____

Materials

microscope
prepared slides of:
  cat ovary, transverse cross section
  rat testis, longitudinal cross section
  rat epididymis, transverse cross section

Safety 🖐

Be careful to avoid breakage when working with glass. Always handle the microscope with extreme care. You are responsible for its proper care and use. Use caution when handling microscope slides as they can break easily and cut you. Note the safety alert symbol in the Procedure and review the meaning of the symbol by referring to Safety Symbols on page 8.

Procedure

Part A. The Mammalian Ovary

🖐 **1.** Obtain a stained slide of a transverse cross section of a mature ovary of a nonpregnant cat. **CAUTION:** *Be careful to handle the slides only by their sides to prevent smearing the sample.* Using the low-power objective of a microscope, focus on a part of the ovary where you can see both the outer edge and the interior of the ovary. The outermost layer of cells of the ovary consists of the germinal epithelium, a single layer of epithelial cells. Immediately below the germinal epithelium is the connective tissue called the stroma. Within the stroma you will observe numerous round structures of various sizes. These structures are the follicles, where the ovarian eggs develop and mature. In some of the follicles you can observe the developing egg, a large, circular cell with a darkly stained nucleus.

2. Examine different areas of the slide under low power to find follicles containing eggs in various stages of development. Using Figure 1 as a guide, trace the development of one developing egg cell. A developing egg is surrounded by a covering, or corona, of follicle cells. As the follicle matures, a cavity filled with the female hormone estrogen develops. Estrogen is essential to the growth and development of the maturing egg. The mature follicle gradually moves to the surface of the ovary, where it ruptures the surface and releases the egg into the Fallopian tube.

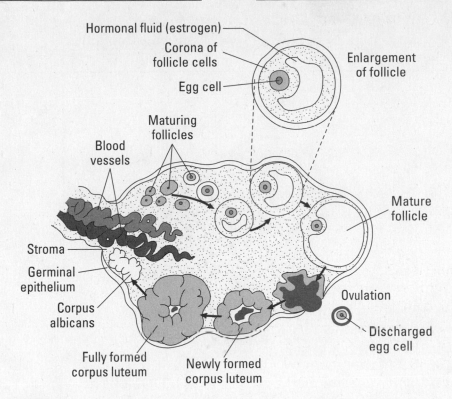

Hormonal fluid (estrogen)

Corona of follicle cells

Egg cell

Enlargement of follicle

Maturing follicles

Blood vessels

Mature follicle

Stroma

Germinal epithelium

Corpus albicans

Ovulation

Discharged egg cell

Fully formed corpus luteum

Newly formed corpus luteum

Figure 1

3. After a follicle ruptures and releases an egg from the ovary, the follicle undergoes a series of changes and becomes an endocrine structure called the corpus luteum. In this process, the follicle cells enlarge and a yellowish substance called lutein accumulates in their cytoplasm. The lutein cells secrete the hormones estrogen and progesterone, which are responsible for building up the lining of the uterus in preparation for pregnancy. Examine a corpus luteum on your slide. If pregnancy does not occur, the corpus luteum continues to grow for about 10 to 12 days and then shrinks, eventually becoming a small, white ovarian scar called a corpus albicans. Locate a corpus albicans on your slide.

Part B. The Mammalian Testis

1. Obtain a stained slide of the testis of a mature rat for examination under the low-power objective of a microscope. The thick outer covering of the testis is called the tunica albuginea. The testis is separated into several wedge-shaped compartments by partitions called septa (singular, *septum*). Examine the cluster of small circles within each compartment. These are the cut surfaces of the tiny, coiled seminiferous tubules, which are involved in the production of sperm. The seminiferous tubules lead into the epididymis, a long, narrow, flattened structure attached to the posterior surface of the testis. Sperm complete their maturation while passing through the epididymis. The lower portion of the epididymis uncoils and widens into a long duct called the vas deferens.

2. In the appropriate place in Figure 2, label the following structures of the testis: tunica albuginea, septa, seminiferous tubules, epididymis, and vas deferens.

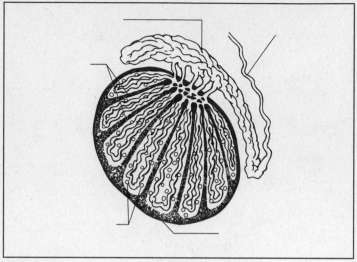

Figure 2   **Rat Testis**

3. Carefully switch to the high-power objective so that you are focusing on one of the seminiferous tubules. **CAUTION:** *When turning to the high-power objective, always look at the objective from the side of the microscope so that the objective does not hit or damage the slide.*

4. Notice that the walls of the seminiferous tubule consist of many layers of cells. The cytoplasm of these cells will most likely be stained red, and the chromosomes in the nuclei will most likely be stained blue. Closely examine these cells in order to trace the various stages of spermatogenesis, or sperm cell production. The cells nearest to the outer surface of the seminiferous tubule are called spermatogonia. These are the sperm-producing cells. The spermatogonia divide by mitosis. Half of the daughter cells remain as spermatogonia, while the other half undergo changes and become cells called primary spermatocytes. The primary spermatocytes make up the layer next to the spermatogonia. Observe the chromosome arrangement in the primary spermatocytes.

5. The diploid primary spermatocyte undergoes the first stage of meiosis, producing two haploid cells called secondary spermatocytes. The secondary spermatocytes are found in a layer next to the primary spermatocytes. The two secondary spermatocytes undergo the second meiotic division, producing four haploid spermatid cells. The spermatid cells make up the innermost layer of the seminiferous tubule. A spermatid cell develops into a sperm with an oval head and a long, whiplike tail.

6. Observe how the sperm cells are clustered around elongated cells that are evenly spaced around the circumference of the seminiferous tubule. These cells, called Sertoli cells, probably provide nutrients for the developing sperm cells. Observe how the sperm cells have their tails facing out into the central opening, or lumen, of the seminiferous tubule.

7. In the appropriate place in Figure 3, label the following parts of the seminiferous tubule: spermatogonia, primary spermatocytes, secondary spermatocytes, spermatids, sperm cells, Sertoli cells, and lumen.

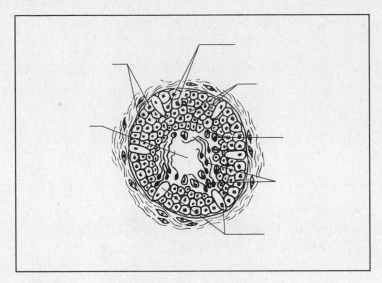

Figure 3   **Rat Seminiferous Tubule**

8. Obtain a prepared slide of a cross section of the epididymis of a mature rat. Observe the epididymis under low and high power. Note the sperm cells clustered within the lumen of the epididymis. Observe that the cells lining the lumen are lined with cilia. These cilia help propel the sperm cells through the epididymis. Observe the smooth muscle cells in the walls of the epididymis. As these muscles contract, the sperm cells are pushed through the epididymis, toward the vas deferens.

9. In the appropriate place in Figure 4, label the following parts of the epididymis: lumen, sperm cells, cilia, and smooth muscle cells.

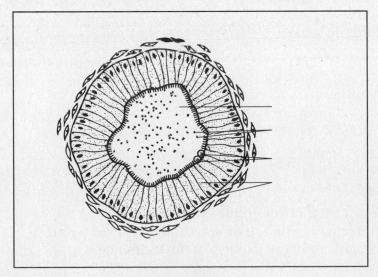

Figure 4   **Rat Epididymis**

Analysis and Conclusions

1. **Comparing and Contrasting** In what way are mature sperm and egg cells different from all other types of body cells?

   _____

2. **Applying Concepts** What is the function of the corpus luteum in the ovary?

   _____

3. **Inferring** What is the adaptive advantage of the tail on the sperm cell?

   _____

4. **Analyzing Data** What are two functions that are common to both ovaries and testes?

   _____

   _____

5. **Comparing and Contrasting** Describe three ways in which sperm-cell development is different from egg-cell development.

   _____

   _____

   _____

6. **Drawing Conclusions** The middle section of a sperm cell is packed with mitochondria. Use your knowledge of cell organelle function to determine the function the mitochondria serve in the sperm cell.

   _____

   _____

   _____

7. **Predicting** What might happen if more than one egg were released at the same time from the ovaries?

   _____

   _____

   _____

8. **Formulating Hypotheses** A mature egg cell contains a great deal more cytoplasm than a mature sperm cell. What is the possible function of the added cytoplasm found within the egg cell?

   _____

Going Further

Research in vitro fertilization through the library and the Internet. Be sure to include information on why the technique is used, what procedures are involved, and how successful the technique is.

Detecting Viruses

Introduction

Some diseases that affect people are caused by viruses. Viruses also cause plant diseases and infect bacteria.

Lysis is an important tool used by virologists to detect the presence of viruses in a cell population. If a culture of bacteria is inoculated with bacteriophages, or viruses that infect bacteria, the lysis of the bacterial cells make the culture appear clear. This clear area is called a plaque. The clearer a phage-infected culture of bacteria is, the greater the number of phages present in the culture.

The culturing of bacteria and bacteriophages requires the use of aseptic, or sterile, techniques. Aseptic techniques prevent contamination of existing cultures by other microorganisms. The heat produced by autoclaving or passing certain materials through the flame of a Bunsen burner is sufficient to destroy microorganisms and keep the environment sterile.

In this investigation, you will inoculate a bacterial culture with a bacteriophage and observe the results. You will also design and carry out an experiment to test for the presence of the same bacteriophage in an unknown suspension.

Problem

How is the presence of bacteriophages in a culture of bacteria determined?

Pre-Lab Discussion

Read the entire investigation. Then, work with a partner to answer the following questions.

1. **Formulating Hypotheses** State a hypothesis that explains the relationship between the presence of bacteriophage and the condition of a bacterial culture.

   _____

   _____

   _____

2. **Controlling Variables** In the procedure performed in Parts A and B, what is the manipulated variable? What is the responding variable?

   _____

   _____

   _____

3. What will happen to the bacteriophage culture as it is transferred from one test tube to the next in Part A, step 12?

   _____

   _____

4. **Predicting** What differences do you expect to see among the five bacteriophage-inoculated lines on the petri dish? Explain the reasons for these differences.

_____

_____

_____

_____

5. **Controlling Variables** What is the control in this experiment? How do you expect the responding variable to behave in the control?

_____

_____

Suggested Materials _(per group)_

Bunsen burner

culture of T-4 bacteriophage

inoculating loop

12 sterile test tubes containing nutrient broth

glass-marking pencil

test-tube rack

nutrient agar plate

culture of _Escherichia coli_

sterile cotton swab

incubator

test tube containing unknown suspension

Request additional materials from your teacher if you
    think you will need them to carry out your experiment.

Safety 🥽🧤🌿🖐️⛏️🔥🗑️🧪⚠️

Put on safety goggles. Put on a laboratory apron if one is available. Be careful to avoid breakage when working with glassware. Always use special caution when working with bacterial cultures. Put on plastic gloves. Follow your teacher's directions and all appropriate safety procedures when handling and disposing of live microorganisms. Tie back loose hair and clothing when working with flames. Do not reach over an open flame. Wash your hands thoroughly after carrying out this investigation. Note all safety alert symbols next to the steps in Design Your Experiment and review the meanings of each symbol by referring to Safety Symbols on page 8.

Design Your Experiment

Part A. Preparing a Bacteriophage Culture

 1. Obtain a culture of T-4 bacteriophage from your teacher.
    CAUTION: _Be very careful when working with microorganisms._

2. Sterilize the inoculating loop by passing it through a Bunsen burner flame as shown in part A of Figure 1. Allow the loop to remain in the flame until the entire length of the wire has turned red. **CAUTION:** *When using a Bunsen burner, wear safety goggles and be sure that hair and loose clothing do not come into contact with the flame. Do not touch the end of the inoculating loop that is placed in the flame or allow it to come into contact with any flammable objects.*

3. While holding the sterile inoculating loop in one hand, pick up in the other hand the test tube containing the T-4 bacteriophage culture and one sterile test tube containing the nutrient broth.

4. Remove the cotton plugs from each test tube by grasping the plugs between the fingers of the hand holding the loop. This technique is shown in part B of Figure 1.

5. Sterilize the mouths of the test tubes by quickly passing them through the flame two or three times as shown in part C of Figure 1.

6. Carefully insert the inoculating loop into the test tube containing the T-4 bacteriophage culture and remove one loopful of culture. **CAUTION:** *Allow the inoculating loop to cool before inserting it into the test tube.*

7. Transfer this loopful of T-4 bacteriophage culture to the test tube containing the nutrient broth.

8. Before replacing the cotton plugs on the two test tubes, sterilize the mouths of the test tubes as you did in step 5. Also, resterilize the inoculating loop. Be sure to replace each plug in the correct test tube.

9. Mix the contents of the test tube containing the nutrient broth and bacteriophage culture by rotating the tube rapidly between your hands. With the glass-marking pencil, label this tube "Stock Phage Culture."

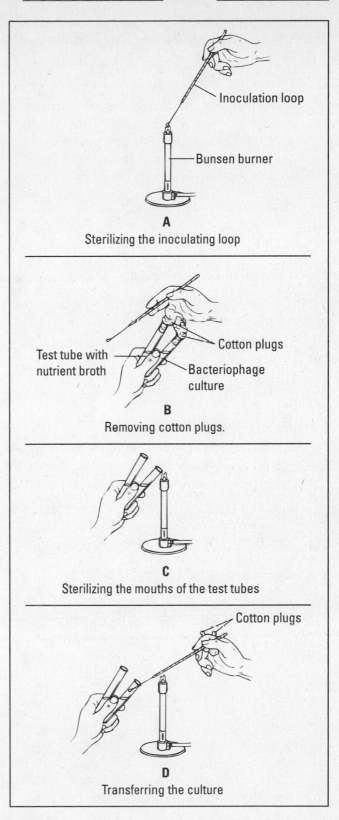

A
Sterilizing the inoculating loop

B
Removing cotton plugs.

C
Sterilizing the mouths of the test tubes

D
Transferring the culture

Figure 1

10. Place five test tubes containing 1 mL each of nutrient broth in a test-tube rack. With the glass-marking pencil, label them 1 through 5.

11. Transfer a loopful of culture from the stock phage culture to test tube 1 following steps 2 through 8.

12. Continue transferring loopfuls from each test tube to the next test tube as shown in Figure 2. Stop when test tube 4 is inoculated. **Note:** *Do not inoculate test tube 5 with the bacteriophage culture.* Wash your hands before continuing with Part B.

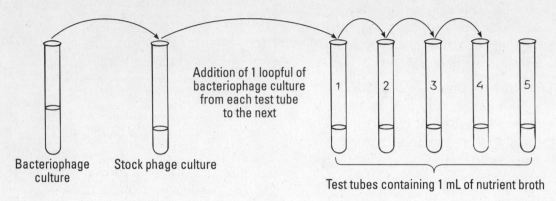

Figure 2

Part B. Growing Bacteria and Bacteriophages on Agar

1. Obtain a nutrient agar plate and turn it upside down. Across the bottom of the plate, draw five lines with the glass-marking pencil. Number each line as shown in Figure 3. Turn the petri dish upright.

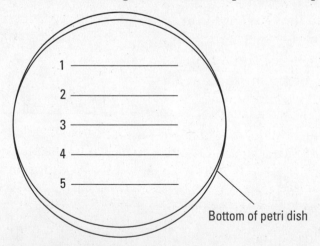

Figure 3

2. Put on plastic gloves. Obtain a culture of *E. coli*. Dip the sterile cotton swab into the culture of *E. coli*.

3. Raise the lid of the petri dish slightly and swab the entire surface of the agar plate with the cotton swab. Try to cover the surface of the agar plate at uniformly as possible.

4. Using the sterile techniques described in steps 2 through 8 of Part A, remove a loopful of material from test tube 1 and streak this on the surface of the nutrient agar plate along line 1. Replace the cotton plug.

5. Follow the same procedure for each of the remaining four test tubes, including test tube 5. Be sure to streak one loopful along the line that corresponds to the test tube number. **Note:** *Be sure to sterilize the loop after each streaking.*

6. After completing the streaking of the bacteriophage dilutions onto the nutrient agar plate, inoculate test tubes 1 through 5 with a loopful of *E. coli* culture. Be sure to follow the sterilization procedures for each inoculation. Mix the contents of each tube well by rapid rotation.

7. Incubate the plate and broth cultures in the incubator at 35° to 37°C.

8. Examine the plate and test tubes after 24 and 48 hours. In Figure 4, sketch what you observe on the agar plate after 24 and 48 hours.

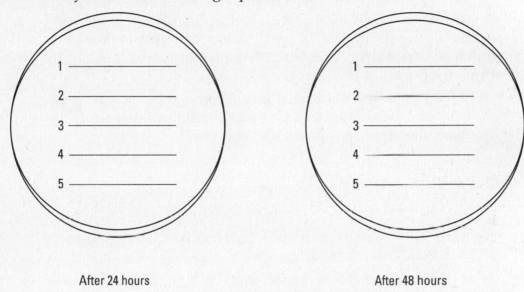

After 24 hours   After 48 hours

Growth of Bacteria on Agar Plate

Figure 4

9. In the Data Table, record the results of your observations after 48 hours. In the first column, use a range of + to indicate minimum plaque formation to ++++ to indicate maximum plaque formation on the agar plate. In the second column, use a range of + for slightly cloudy to ++++ for maximum cloudiness in the test tubes.

10. Return the agar plate and test tubes to your teacher for proper disposal. **CAUTION:** *Wash your hands thoroughly with soap and water.*

Data Table

Test Tube	Plaque formation (clearing on streaks)	Growth of E. coli (cloudiness in test tubes)
1		
2		
3		
4		
5		

Part C. Your Own Experiment

1. You have learned how to prepare viral and bacterial cultures using aseptic techniques. In this third part of the investigation, you will be given a test tube that may or may not contain bacteriophage. You will design an experiment to determine whether or not bacteriophage is present in the test tube.

2. Consider how the presence of bacteriophage was determined in parts A and B of this investigation. Can you detect the presence of bacteriophage directly or is it its presence inferred?

   _____
   _____
   _____
   _____
   _____

3. Design an experiment that will demonstrate the absence or presence of T-4 bacteriophage in an unknown suspension. Begin by formulating a hypothesis. Describe the results you expect to see if your hypothesis is supported. Describe the experimental results you expect to see if your hypothesis is *not* supported.

   Hypothesis

   _____
   _____
   _____
   _____
   _____

   Prediction

   _____
   _____
   _____
   _____
   _____

⚠ 4. In the lines below, write down your experimental plan for submission to your teacher. Note your manipulated, responding, and control variables. List the materials you will use and any safety precautions you should follow. Write the procedure you will use as numbered steps. Submit your experimental plan to your teacher for approval. When your teacher approves your plan, carry out your experiment. Record your data in an appropriate format on a separate sheet of paper.

_____

_____

_____

_____

_____

_____

_____

_____

Manipulated variable

_____

Responding variable

_____

_____

Controlled variables

_____

_____

Materials

_____

Safety Precautions

_____

_____

Procedure

_____

_____

_____

_____

_____

_____

_____

Analysis and Conclusions

1. **Designing Experiments** What were the manipulated and responding variables in your experiment, and how did you evaluate (or quantify) them?

_____

_____

_____

_____

_____

2. **Controlling Variables** What was a controlled variable in your experiment?

_____

_____

3. **Observing** Summarize the results of your experiment.

_____

_____

_____

4. **Analyzing Data** Do your results support your hypothesis or contradict it?

_____

_____

_____

_____

5. **Drawing Conclusions** How strongly do your results support your conclusion? Explain your answer.

_____

_____

_____

_____

Going Further

To determine whether viruses are filterable, obtain a microbiological filter from your teacher and filter the contents of test tube 4. Using the inoculating loop and aseptic techniques, inoculate test tube 5 with the filtered material and incubate the test tube at 35° to 37°C for 24 hours. What do you observe in test tube 5? What conclusions can you make?